VERMONT WILD

Adventures of Vermont Fish & Game Wardens

VOLUME 1

MEGAN
PRICE

VERMONT WILD

Adventures of Vermont Fish & Game Wardens

VOLUME 1

Written by **Megan Price**

Stories by **Eric Nuse**

Illustrated by **Bob Lutz**

Pine Marten Press

Pine Marten Press

Third edition

Copyright © 2011 by Megan Price

Printed in the USA.

For information and book orders, visit our website:
www.PineMartenPress.com

ISBN: 978-0-9828872-1-9

Library of Congress Control Number: 2010934765

Answers to your most pressing questions:

Did the stories in this book actually happen?
Yes. We couldn't make this stuff up.

Have the stories been embroidered just a little?
A whole lot less than most fishin' and huntin' stories.

What about the characters?
The characters are composites – bits and pieces of many individuals. In most instances we have used wardens' and innocent bystanders' actual first names, but only after they swore up and down they wouldn't sue us.

The poachers' names and physical descriptions are fabricated. But the scofflaws' actions and convictions are real.

Why did you fudge names and characters?
Vermont is a small state.
We want to continue to live here.

Aren't Vermont cruisers green?
How come Eric is driving a red one?
Eric was assigned a red cruiser for a time for investigations. We thought a red car on the cover would get more people to pick up the book and help us sell more copies.
You did *buy* this book, right?

Get ready, here it comes...

Disclaimer
Any resemblance to any individual,
living or dead, is one heck of a coincidence.

That's our story and we're sticking to it.

Dedication

This book is dedicated
to our families and friends
and
to all who work to protect
wildlife and wild places.

Ten Percent

Ten percent of all profits
will be used for wildlife protection
and outdoor education.

VERMONT WILD
Volume 2
with more great warden stories is available now.
Visit www.PineMartenPress.com
to learn more.

STORIES

Fishin' Tackle 1

Raccoon Riot 19

Mongo 41

Clyde River Race 65

Hunt 'Er Up 79

Furry Fish Finder 99

Bear? *WHERE???* 115

Squish in the Night 135

Thin Ice 147

Too Loose Moose 169

Moose Vesuvius 195

Gimmee the Gun 223

Cover Me 247

"Marty's hands flew up into the air
and he high stepped it like a carthorse
stung by a bee. With his first big step
he threw down his fly rod. With his
second step he leaned forward and
opened his creel – spilling its contents
into the rock-strewn river. I saw a
rainbow of small silver fish splash
into the water and slide
across the rocks."

Fishin' Tackle

Whenever folks start talking about fishing tackle, my mind drifts away from plastic crawlers, spoons, spinner baits and other lures. I think back to one of my first days in uniform and an honest-to-gosh, real fishing tackle.

I was a warden trainee in the Green Mountain state, just starting off on my career and learning from one of the best, Warden Denny G. Denny was a big, likable guy with a ready laugh and a reputation for tough. A former Marine, Denny had not lost any of his edge despite being a dozen plus years out of the Corps. He took just as much pride in being a Vermont Fish and Game warden as he did being a Marine. He worked himself and his trainees hard.

It was my first week on the job and Denny was introducing me to the Wagon Wheel area of Ripton. Locals know the area as home to poet Robert Frost's cabin. Most every American school child reads Frost's poem "The Road Not

Taken" at some point and is asked to analyze it. Denny, it seemed to me, had a real affinity with the old poet. He insisted on taking me and all his other trainees on roads we didn't even know existed.

This area is popular for its hardy native brook trout population and good deer hunting. I was told it was named the Wagon Wheel because a lot of deer trails come together there—like spokes—to the center hub.

Hiking into the Wagon Wheel can be treacherous. There are boulders, steep hillsides, dark mossy ledge and forest overhanging tiny mountain streams. Make a mistake and you can fall 50 feet before you slam into the rocks below. Forget walking out with a bum leg. If you slip in some spots, you'll be leaving on a gurney with pallbearers for company.

There are a couple easier ways into the Wagon Wheel, but Denny didn't take them. In fact, you could drive right up to within a few feet of some nice fishing holes. But again, that wasn't Denny's style. A day in the woods with Denny was a serious work out.

It was early spring and the thought was there would be some fishermen along the back country streams angling for native trout, despite patches of snow in the deep woods. Locals call them "brookies." Because these native fish are small and increasingly rare, the daily limit is small too. It can be tempting for a greedy angler to take more than the law allows.

Denny and I spied a truck tucked off a log road a couple miles back as we hiked in. You can kinda tell if a truck belongs to a native or a newcomer. Most Vermont natives still drive American made trucks. And their bumper stickers are often not just politically incorrect but sometimes designed to shock fellow drivers.

In a kind of reverse status symbol, it is a badge of honor to have an old truck covered in bondo, rust, dents and mud. This truck had all that and more. The indications were the owner was more likely to be a NRA lifetime member than a bird watcher. A peek through the truck's windows disclosed some empty Snell hook packs on the bench seat. Brookie sized. Yup, gone fishing.

Well, what Denny had now was a chance for his young trainee to practice greeting and meeting the public.

It didn't take us but five minutes to locate a guy about 50 years old fishing the brook.

Denny and I were wearing our badges and he let me take the lead on introductions. I knew he wanted to see how I handled myself.

I checked the man's license and it was good. Then I asked to see his creel. He pursed his lips, lowered his head. He wasn't too happy to hand it over. He had a half dozen brookies in there. That was okay. Trouble was, four out of the six were under sized and therefore illegal and he knew it.

He wasn't shy about his crime.

This fellow flat out told us he and his buddy, who owned the truck, had come to get a bunch of native trout for a fish fry and they had agreed before they set out they would keep whatever bit their hooks.

He claimed brookies were the best eating fish, said he was a native, born and raised here and he'd leave the flatlanders and the tourists the big, lazy, farm bred stocked trout swimming in rivers closer to town.

While his honesty was refreshing, his attitude was not. We seized his fish, took his license and sent him back to the truck and told him to stay put. Then we began a search for his fishing partner.

Ten minutes later, Denny and I spotted the other fellow, knee deep in the middle of the stream about 30 yards up ahead of us, casting his line back and forth towards a sweet spot on the opposite shore.

Denny hollered over the sound of the brook, "Hey Marty, how's the fishing?"

Hunh, I thought. Guess Denny knows this guy. I stood a few feet from Denny expecting the angler to give a big wave and smile back.

But the fellow showed no reaction. He just kept fishing. He was pretending he didn't even see us. Denny was a big man and there was no way you'd miss him. I'm no shadow myself. But the guy just made another big cast and with it, took a bigger step closer to the far shore—deftly moving away from us.

"Marty, we just sent your fishing partner back to the truck. We need to look at your license and check your catch now," Denny yelled upstream to the angler.

The "I don't hear or see you" game continued. Marty sent out another smooth cast, his back to us.

Denny scowled and walked to the edge of the brook, with me a step behind like a good bird dog awaiting orders. Denny called again to Marty, making a bit of small talk and edged closer. Marty continued to pretend he was deaf.

I could hear the exasperation growing in Denny's voice and saw the cords in his neck start to tighten.

Like me, it had not escaped Denny that Marty was inching slowly away, casting over into little pools at the far side. The river was a good forty feet wide across this section and the water was fast. Some of those pools would be eight or more feet deep. Nice fishing, but a little treacherous.

If Marty made a break for it up the bank and into the woods, he might just be able to escape. Denny sighed, looked over his right shoulder at me, and gave me a nod. I understood this was my signal to go after Marty.

Denny shouted above the sound of the rushing water. "Marty, Eric is coming over to see you."

The toe of my boot had barely hit the water when Marty blew up like a flushed grouse. His peripheral vision, his hearing, or both had miraculously improved.

Marty's hands flew up into the air and he high stepped it like a carthorse stung by a bee. With

his first big step he threw down his fly rod.
With his second step he leaned forward and
opened his creel—spilling its contents into the
rock-strewn river. I saw a rainbow of small
silver fish splash into the water and slide across
the rocks.

Free of his gear, Marty high tailed it for the bank
and began clawing his way up through the sand
and saplings into a dark pine grove.

The race was on.

I bent my knees slightly and spread my arms
out wide like a tight rope walker with a fear of
heights.

I tried to dance my way across the racing water.
It was a mess of mossy-topped rocks, ankle
busting glass slick cobbles topped with rotting
tree trunks and roots.

I was hopping, skittering and slogging as fast
as my boots would allow trying my best not to
fall in.

My first stop was where Marty had dumped
his creel. I wanted to save the evidence and I
needed to mark the spot.

I bent down for a quick look.

I counted more than a dozen belly-up brookies swirling in a small whirlpool between some boulders. I knew there would be more down stream.

I set my hat down on the biggest rock to mark the spot and picked up a few of the dead fish and set them beside it. I didn't want all my evidence washing away.

Then I gritted my teeth and looked about for the guy doing the damage here. He was on the far side of the stream looking back at me over his shoulder.

When we made eye contact, he reared up and shot off again.

Marty might be stepping as high as a Morgan horse at the Tunbridge Fair, but I knew he couldn't keep that pace up for long. If I could stay on his trail, I would catch him eventually.

I had to. I sure didn't want to face Denny if I lost him.

Marty raised his rubbery legs up to his chest like a show horse. He trotted the final few yards splashing and puffing for shore. His arms were flapping like a fat, flustered hen.

I lit out after him, dancing from rock to rock trying to plot a path through the white water and swift currents. I was a reluctant hound on the trail.

It was too much for Denny.

From behind me I could hear his chuckle followed by a knee slap and a "Sic 'em, Eric!" then a pause and more and louder laughter.

I was glad somebody thought this was funny. I could fall and break my neck any second. I had just bought new boots, new pants and a new shirt too. Like a kid in the first week of school, I wasn't looking forward to ruining my clothes so early in the year and having to explain this to my mom—or in this case—my wife.

I had sized Marty up at the beginning of the race and figured it would not take much to wear him down. He was at least 25 years older than me and out of shape. Unless I fell and broke my leg or split my head open, I should be able to nab him.

I let Marty get a good start on me, in part to allow him to tire himself out. I didn't want this to turn into a fist fight in the rushing waters. If we got into a tussle and he or I fell back onto those river rocks halfway up the bank, one or

both of us could bust a rib, or worse, our skulls.
I figured the smartest thing for me to do was let
him run until the fight was out of him.

In between rock jumping I was still seeing dead
brookies floating past. I kept a running count in
my head and kept jumping from rock to rock.

I looked up just in time to see Marty scramble
up the bank and into the pines. I lost sight of
him for a bit.

Behind me, above the sound of the rushing
water, I heard Denny still egging me on.

"Halt!" I yelled to Marty as he headed into the
trees. I don't know why I thought he might stop,
but I figured I should try it.

I made it to shore in one piece and pulled myself
up the bank with the help of some saplings.
Once I got into the pine stand, I stood and
listened for a few seconds.

Away from the rushing brook, it was much
easier to hear. I heard branches snapping up
ahead. I trotted towards the sound.

Within a minute I saw him—his prance was now
a stagger and Marty was reaching for his side
like a runner out of oxygen.

He was almost out of the pines, headed into a small clearing of chest high grass, last winter's weeds and a big tangle of berry bushes off to the right. Just a few more steps and I could grab him.

"Stop!" I yelled when I was 50 feet behind him.

He was like an old toy winding down—making the same arm and leg motions, but at half the speed of a few minutes earlier.

He would not give up.

I shook my head in disbelief. I ran until I was trotting beside Marty. I screamed into his ear, "STOP!"

Marty looked straight ahead, tucked his double chins tight to his chest like an angry bull and scooted right. He plunged into that big mess of last summer's berry bushes like a moose. I guess he figured I wouldn't follow. Of course, he had waders on to protect his legs. And he was sporting a good, thick wool shirt too.

I was dressed for a pleasant spring outing in my trainee khakis and a pressed cotton shirt. Here were chest high bushes with thorns the size of steak knife blades coming at me and I couldn't do a darn thing about it.

Even a bear would think twice about going into that tangle. He'd at least have to close his eyes.

I felt like a beagle on a rabbit track. The rabbit goes into the berry bushes, you gotta go too. It was just part of the job.

Dang this guy.

I closed my eyes, gritted my teeth and dove in after Marty. I felt my arms and ribs and legs being ripped by thorns, heard the "rrrrrrrrrrip!" of a thousand barbs tearing at my pants and shirt sleeves.

I was about to be a fish fillet myself unless I stopped him.

I decided a tackle was in order. I slammed into Marty with my right shoulder and hip doing my best impersonation of an NFL tackle.

There was an "umph" and an "oh" and then a big dull whomp when we hit the ground, with me lying on top of a big pile of crumpled green waders.

"Stop! Stop, I've got you," I hissed in Marty's ear and I sat up and reached for his hands. Still not so much as a glance my way from this guy and not a word. He lay there like a tasered tuna.

Amazing. Maybe he was so short of breath he couldn't talk.

"You're under arrest," I growled.

It was all Marty could do to breathe. He was all done in from his brook and brush dance. I stood up and looked hard at the guy for the first time. I saw I had middle aged poacher with a beer gut and from the smell of him, a bad smoking habit. A busted up pack of Camels had squeezed out of his breast pocket in the tackle and lay atop last summer's milkweed pods, like toothpaste from a tube.

"Okay, I am going to pat you down for weapons, then you are going to get up. Don't do anything stupid," I added, while thinking, "It's a little late for that."

I gave Marty an additional few seconds on the ground to catch his breath and then helped him get to his feet. I didn't want a poacher with a heart attack on my hands. We started back to the river.

I had no problem finding our way—all I had to do was follow the trail of trampled winter grasses and busted branches.

Denny tried to look stern as I poked my head

out of the brush with Marty stumbling ahead of me in handcuffs. But as soon as he saw the condition of my new uniform, he couldn't contain himself.

"Eric, did you run into a bear in those bushes?" Denny shouted across the water.

I looked down and saw my left pant leg was split along the inside seam from my crotch to my boot, several shirt buttons were missing and the elbow of my new shirt was torn out, too.

So much for my first week of school clothes, I thought.

I took off Marty's cuffs and carefully escorted him across the brook over to Denny. I didn't want him falling in and getting hurt. But walking him across the stream meant I had to walk through the icy current for most of the crossing rather than jump from boulder to boulder. Forget dry boots. Forget dry anything. I was soaked by the time I got him across.

I handed Marty over to Denny, then I slogged back through the brook once more to gather up the evidence Marty had left behind.

All around my hat were dying and dead brook trout. I counted nearly three dozen—many under the minimum length. Marty was smart. He had opened the lid on his creel and dumped it hoping the evidence would wash away down stream. But the river had held most of his illegal catch. The dead and dying brookies were floating in the pools trapped between the boulders. The evidence was compelling and shameful. No wonder Marty ran.

I scooped up the dead fish and put them in an evidence bag wardens carry with them for just such occasions. Then, I took a few more steps and picked up Marty's smashed creel and fly rod. With all the evidence in hand, I slogged back through the water to Denny one last time. I showed my boss the evidence bag and gave him my count.

There was no more smile on Denny's face. Marty had done real damage to the fish population on this popular brook. "You're done, Marty," Denny said, "Let's go." And we marched him back out to the pick up truck where his buddy was waiting.

Both Marty and his buddy were cited to appear in court and we took their rods, creels, licenses and the fish as evidence.

Then, like a true Marine, Denny chose to have us hike back out of the Wagon Wheel to his cruiser the long, hard way. We could have ridden out at least part of the way with the poachers. He could have chosen a flatter route to walk me out. My feet were becoming prunes in my boots. But where was the fun in that?

Maybe Denny decided we should hike back out so my clothes would have a chance to dry. Maybe he didn't want anyone seeing me with him when my uniform looked like a bear had mauled me. I don't know. He never said. And I might have been green, but I knew enough not to ask.

I hiked out of there with my split pant leg foh-wapping, foh-wapping with every step. My undies were shining like a whitetail too. Sure wished I had brought some safety pins with me.

Denny and I froze up the brookies and stored the scofflaws' rods, reels and creels for evidence and waited for the trial. Of course, we had to go back to the office to do the paperwork and all the other guys got to see me looking like I had been trampled by a buffalo—a water buffalo. I was still a little damp and literally itching to get my boots off and find some dry socks.

When I came through the door that night, my wife was some put out by the condition of my new uniform. My new shirt was beyond repair.

It was reduced to mow-the-lawn-and-change-
the-oil status. The good news was my trousers
were salvageable. They had torn along the
inside seam. A careful run through the sewing
machine fixed them.

As for Marty, he stayed silent right to the end.
He hired an attorney who, once he saw the
evidence we had against his client, pled guilty
and saved us the trouble of going to trial. Marty
and his buddy each paid a hefty fine and their
fishing licenses were revoked for a year.

Best of all, I earned some points within the
Department as a warden trainee who wasn't
afraid to leap right into the water, chase
down and even tackle a poacher if necessary.

Denny had a good time telling the story about
his new warden trainee and for a week or so my
nickname was "Fishin' Tackle" Nuse.

I've been called worse, but I was happy that
particular nickname didn't stick.

"A shudder went through me,
not because of that one angry baby
coon perched at my shoulder, but
because I felt a furry brush race across
the hair on the back of my neck."

Raccoon Riot

Before Vermont adopted the use of wildlife rehabilitators, it was up to local wardens like me to make the call on what to do with lost or orphaned babies. All of us did our best to get the animals back into the wild.

I would place orphaned babies with good people who had the skill and patience to nurture these critters until they were old enough to make it on their own. Then I would return and pick them up and drive the orphans to a suitable release area I had scoped out a few days earlier. I made certain there would be enough food and cover for them to thrive.

I developed a pretty good network of volunteers and many of them specialized in one species or another. For instance, my deputy's wife, Jackie, had a talent for rearing fox kits and coyote pups, the state conservation camp counselors did an exceptional job with fawns, and the guys over at the Boy Scout camp in

Eden liked raising baby raccoons and were
good at it. Maybe the fun loving, I'll-try-most-
anything, enthusiasm of the camp counselors
matched that of wide-eyed orphaned raccoon
babies. Whatever, it worked.

And that is where I was headed this fine July
morning, over to Eden to pick up eight baby
raccoons. The coons had lost their mom to a
speeding driver. I had scooped up the babies
and dropped them off weeks earlier, when
each was nothing more than a tiny handful of
squinting, tumbling striped fur. There are not
many babies that are cuter at that age. Now
approaching 12 weeks old these baby raccoons
were still cute as the dickens, but they were
tough as steel springs and as lively as jumping
beans. It was a full-time job keeping them out of
mischief.

They could have been climbing the walls of the
bunkhouses, wadding up and chewing sheets
and pillows, rifling through campers' duffle bags
looking for treats and scampering around like
kittens on steroids. But the counselors had
learned long ago about the inquisitive nature of
baby raccoons and had built a spacious kennel
outfitted with tree limbs and toys. The wire cage
did a good job of containing the raccoon orphans
while entertaining them as well.

I took one look at the orphans presented to me and agreed they were healthy, vigorous and capable of fending for themselves. It was time to move them to the woods and hope they would forget what a great deal they had going with the humans. They needed to learn to be independent. Adult raccoons are strong, smart and stubborn. They are a formidable adversary—just ask a coon dog. Adult raccoons have been known to kill dogs three and more times their size.

I had chosen a spot about 20 miles down the road from the camp for the coons' new home. The drive wouldn't take too long. While the counselors were saying their final goodbyes, I went to dig my folding dog crate from the trunk of my cruiser.

Dang, it wasn't there.

Then I remembered I had used it to deliver a sick heron to a wildlife vet a few days earlier. I got to talking and must have forgotten to take the cage and put it back in my trunk.

Lucky for me the counselors found a good-sized cardboard box. We loaded eight cute as the dickens raccoon babies—some chattering, some sleeping, some clawing at the air with all four feet like they were swimming for shore—into the box. I folded the top shut and tucked it into the back seat of my cruiser, said my goodbyes, thanked them for another job well done, put the cruiser in drive and headed out.

The sun was warming up the July sky fast. It was a bit past 10 am, so I rolled my window down and leaned over to the passenger side to spin that window down too, before I fired up the engine. No power anything in this state-assigned vehicle. Air conditioning was also courtesy of Mother Nature.

I wanted to move these little guys into the woods before the sun was noon hot to lessen any heat related stress on their little bodies and allow them to acclimate themselves to their new home as early in the day as possible.

I knew the woods would be a good 10 to 15 degrees cooler once we got under the tree canopy.

With the coons stashed in the box in the back seat, my left elbow crooked out the driver's window, we headed over East Hill in Eden, me humming a tune and pausing now and again to talk nonsense to the babies in the box, in an attempt to comfort them.

There was scratching and chirping inside the box behind me and I considered that a good sign. Before long I was just humming along—me and the cruiser—with the sound of eight baby raccoons scratching the inside of the cardboard box, chattering and tumbling there in the back seat.

Two miles or so into our journey, I paused to try and remember the next verse to the song I was singing and I noticed something—silence. The scratching had stopped inside the box.

Uh oh.

Like the old joke in the cowboy movies, it was quiet—too quiet.

I looked into the rear view mirror and saw a flash of black and silver. There was a tiny masked bandit standing on his hind legs on the rear seat ledge, his front claws scraping at the glass. Then another movement caught my eye, this one a lot closer. Looking back at me in the rear view mirror was what appeared to be a BIG raccoon.

He was next to my right shoulder and his shiny black button eyes were glaring at me. His nails dug deep into the seat fabric. It was a shock seeing these big eyes in a mask staring at me from the mirror. I jumped and inadvertantly yanked the wheel and the cruiser swerved.

When I opened my eyes a split second later, I saw the raccoon was holding on for dear life and rocking back and forth with the motion of the cruiser. He looked more angry than afraid. I was just hoping he didn't grab onto my ear to steady himself. It was the closest handle he could grab.

A shudder went through me, not because of that one angry baby coon perched at my shoulder, but because I felt a furry brush race across the hair on the back of my neck. It was another raccoon. This one was skittering along the top of the back seat, bobbing his head up and down, trying to get a fix on the passing scenery. Maybe he felt like a raccoon rocket jockey, with the trees moving so fast before his eyes.

My head was on a swivel looking for loose coons. They were popping up everywhere in the vehicle now. And outside, the road traffic was picking up as well. When I looked in the rear view mirror again, I saw I had a work truck riding my bumper and a grizzled driver waving his fist at me.

I decided I had to quit counting raccoons and
drive the car. I stuck my arm out the window
and waved the truck past me and pulled off to
the side of the road.

My right front tire hit a pothole and what had
been a relatively quiet bunch of loose baby coons
immediately changed. Suddenly the cruiser was
awash with the sounds of chattering teeth, tiny
claws tearing into taxpayer-owned seat fabric,
and a series of thumps and bumps as they
ricocheted over the interior like animated ping
pong balls.

I had a raccoon riot on my hands.

I yanked the wheel to the left and got the cruiser
back up onto the main road and hit the gas
pedal hard. I thought a stiffer breeze might
knock the little marauders back into the box or
at least slow them down—like beach walkers
facing a hurricane force wind.

The surge in speed stopped the little coon
that had brushed my neck from continuing to
skitter along the top of the car seat behind me.
Or maybe it was the G force wind coming in
through the front side windows. Now, he was
perched tight beside my right ear holding on
for dear life. He was so close his whiskers were
tickling my cheek.

Since he was holding still so nicely, I took
the opportunity to take my right hand off the
steering wheel and reach up and over my
shoulder in a nice slow arc to nab him. I got
behind his head all right and grabbed him and
pulled up. But his claws were sunk into the
car seat fabric like porcupine quills. After two
good tugs, I realized he was not going to let go
and all I was doing was making him mad. I let
him go.

Okay, friend. Just sit tight and hold on. You
can be my copilot. Just don't bite that ear.

Then I saw a flash of gray and black to my left
and felt something go running across my lap.
I realized the raccoon at my ear was the least of
my problems now. His buddies had infiltrated
the cockpit and were going in low.

I glanced down and saw I had three or four
raccoons in the front of the cruiser with me.
One was standing on the front passenger door
armrest, stretching as high as he could to catch
the breeze, nose sniffing the air like a hound
dog puppy. The one that had run across my
lap was now wrestling with a pal on the seat
beside me.

Then something bumped my left foot and I heard

scratching on the floor mat. I took my foot off the gas and spread my knees to see another coon rolling around the floor with a plastic bag in its mouth. He was headed towards the brake and gas pedals.

This rascal had found the remains of a half eaten peanut butter and jelly sandwich I had stuffed beneath the front seat a week or more ago, intending to put it in the trash. He was in heaven, tearing and biting into the grimy contents and chirruping as he tumbled and kicked with his hind feet. I saw peanut butter on a pink tongue and paws. I twisted my left foot around him in a soccer move I saw in high school and pushed him gently up and away from the gas and brake pedals. He just kept chewing and clawing and didn't seem the least upset about my size 11 boots sliding him across the floor mat.

Well, at least this one is busy and content and out of my way, I thought. I pressed my right foot on the gas pedal again. In another few minutes I could set them free.

Just then I saw a dark cloud approaching over my head. It was another baby—this one was walking shakily across the cruiser's headliner, hanging upside down. His fur was out straight

like a terrified cat and his eyes were the size
of silver dollars—a kind of hairy raccoon-
spider. His tail was swiping at my face like a
furry windshield wiper. I ducked and cringed,
the cruiser swerved again, but the orphan just
swayed like a pendulum and held on.

He was headed towards the windshield.
Apparently, he or she had no idea which end
was up. I leaned to the left and reached up with
my right hand to pry the astronaut coon off the
headliner. Unlike his friend who was still sitting
next to my collar, this one was more than willing
to let go. He fell on his back right into my palm.
I gave him a gentle toss to the back seat and
stepped on the gas. I had another 10 miles or so
to go to my chosen release site and I didn't want
to think of the next trick these babies might
pull.

As the cruiser picked up speed, it struck me that
the sound in the back seat had changed. It was
no longer the little scratching sounds of claws on
cardboard. It sounded more like claws and teeth
ripping into fabric.

Oh no! I grabbed the rear view mirror and
angled it down, leaned forward and stuck my
nose about onto the mirrored glass. I saw two
coons were now biting and tearing into my

lunch bag and a third was intent on destroying the fabric and vinyl of the back seat itself. Those little teeth could do some real damage.

I was about half way to my planned release site. How much more damage could those coon babies get into in another ten minutes? How would I explain the damage to the cruiser to my boss if they did?

I was considering my options when something new caught my eye over my left shoulder. A wide-eyed baby coon had smelled the breeze and decided to make a break for it. He had jumped half way through my open window. His front paws were resting on the side view mirror and his back feet were on the narrow door ledge resting on the window glass. He was hunkering down and appeared ready to jump into the road.

Darn it!

I let loose of the steering wheel with my left hand and made a grab for the wild child whose fluffy tail was out straight. I guess he figured it would serve as a parachute. He was headed for the pavement.

I said I would save these coons and I was going

to do it if it killed me. I snagged him by the tail and pulled back into the cab. He gave an angry squeak as I tossed him into the back seat. I was certain he wasn't hurt. He just didn't like having his plans changed.

I began rolling up my windows before some of the other bandits got the same prison break idea.

So much for Mother Nature's air conditioning. I might as well have been in the cardboard box with 'em. With the windows rolled up, the coon crew now decided my body was the place to be. I suppose they were scared and humans meant safety, like momma coon, in a scary place.

I had one crawling up my left pant leg, two on my lap fighting and one crawling over my shirt collar. I felt another bump on my left boot and heard a baby growl. I looked down to see the coon tearing into the grimy sandwich had been joined by another baby. They were wrestling for it. Well, at least I knew where most of them were. I always do try to look on the bright side of things. I used my left boot to brush them back whenever they rolled near the brake pedal—which was about every two seconds.

It seemed to me, with the windows closed and

the temperature rising outdoors, the smell of raccoons was getting a little thick.

A guy in a beater pickup with duct taped fenders was rattling towards us in the opposite lane. Two baby raccoons skittered across my dashboard and the coon copilot that had been sitting at my shoulder was now sitting on top of my head. His hind feet dug into the top of my ears.

It's a challenge to surprise most Vermonters up here in the Northeast Kingdom. We routinely see everything from deer and moose tied to car hoods and roof racks to all manner of Grapes of Wrath homemade transportation. But a live Davey Crockett coon skin cap wriggling on top of my head and another half dozen of them bouncing around the cruiser produced a look of astonishment on this fellow's face as he drove by.

I was sweating now—a combination of the July sun, closed driver's window and a good dose of anxiety at my situation—but a few seconds later I got a lot wetter.

What the....?

I reached for the back of my head and ran my right hand down into my collar where something was dripping. As I pulled my hand back to my face to take a look, my nose took a sniff and my eyes caught a good look and my stomach flipped. I shuddered and gagged.

The little darling on top of my head had deposited a loose load of baby excrement there. What was not sitting on my right hand was sliding down the back of my neck and headed down my spine into my boxers.

Dang it! This was bad.

Coon leap or no coon leap, I rolled my driver's window down and threw my head out into the fresh air to stop myself from throwing up inside the cab and my right foot went hard for the brake. I couldn't take it anymore. Time to raise the white flag.

Maybe the raccoons didn't much like how I smelled either. I don't know. But spying the open window and a fresh breath of air—or maybe celebrating their success in partially disabling their captor—the coons that had been skittering across the dash made a break for it.

They leaped, tumbled, rolled, bounced and chattered up and across my bent back, along my neck and through my hair. My copilot coon was knocked off my head and into the grass, whether he wanted to go or not. I felt a series of bounding little feet and was helpless to stop 'em. My thick skull was being used as a launch pad. Some just leapt and were gone. One or two dug their claws hard into my scalp and wriggled to get set before jumping into the grass.

I was helpless. I lolled my tongue out the window and gagged and gagged again. It was as if I had been hit by tear gas. I couldn't breathe.

When my head came up, I saw through teary eyes that one coon baby had slid all the way down the cruiser hood, his four feet wrapped around the hood ornament. He was hanging on for dear life. His buddy had buried his hind feet in the windshield wiper well and was watching me retch and drool.

I couldn't tell if they were concerned for my welfare or just laughing at me. The windshield wiper coon took a good long look at me through the glass. When he saw me come up for air, I guess he decided I was going to be all right. Or maybe he decided I was no longer entertaining. I saw him turn his head towards the woods. His buddies were calling. He was going with them. When the hood ornament coon saw the windshield coon run, he let loose his grip too, fell to the ground and skittered off into the high grass.

I took a deep gulp of fresh air. My eyes were clearing a bit. All thoughts of reaching the perfect raccoon release point left me. This was survival we were talking about now—mine.

I looked up and saw this appeared to be a perfect spot to release raccoons. It was not a shopping mall parking lot. There were no packs of dogs foaming at the mouth waiting to be unleashed on them. There were trees. What else did they need?

I reached behind me and threw on my flashers, blue lights, yellows and any and all other colors I had available but kept my head outside in the fresh air. I looked right and left and saw there were no vehicles approaching.

I opened my driver's door wide. The light and air prompted the two little darlings who had been wrestling at my feet over the shredded peanut butter sandwich to stop their fighting, stand up on their hind legs and sniff the air. They clawed all the way up my pant legs towards my groin and perched in my lap looking out the door.

They were undecided as to whether they should go out into the big wide world or not.

I lifted my leg outside the door and gave them a gentle push forward with my forearm. They dropped to the brushy roadside with cat-like precision and waddled off in classic raccoon style. They chattered and bounced their way towards the tree line. I sighed and looked around for more coons.

Silence. Blessed silence. They were all gone.

I was just starting to regain my serenity when I began to notice the smell inside the cruiser. It wasn't just my head and neck they had used as a latrine. I glanced down at my trousers and along the dash and the front seat and it wasn't at all pretty.

The evidence suggested the camp counselors had given these babies an exceptionally big breakfast with all the trimmings before they packed 'em up in the goodbye box. All that good feed had been expeditiously processed and deposited all over my cruiser as a parting gift.

It was my turn to bolt out of the car. I had been peed and pooped on and my cruiser smelled bad—like it had been soaked in god-awful, concentrated raccoon urine.

I hoped to God no one was watching me stumble out of the cruiser bent over and gagging. My face, neck, arms and legs, even my scalp was scratched up and bleeding from the miniature steak knife claws of those baby coons and my clothes were damp with baby coon pee and worse.

I desperately wanted to rip off my shirt and pants and run into the woods, find a brook and jump in.

I popped open the trunk of the cruiser and dug around for a jug of water and a rag I kept there. I poured half the jug over my head, then used the rest to wash and scrub my shirt and pants before daring to look inside the cruiser.

There was a smear of peanut butter and jelly and torn bread and the remnants of the sandwich bag on the driver's floor mat, pee and poop and wet paw prints all over the dash and rear window sill, more smeared paw prints on all the windows, the front and back seats, even the headliner. My gear in the back seat was chewed, scratched and had some mysterious wet spots as well.

When a car or truck would drive by, I turned to face the open trunk and ducked down to pretend

I was very busy. I was hiding. I prayed nobody stopped and wanted to chat. I was a stinking mess.

I could see I was going to need a lot more water, a lot more rags and a good dose of Pine Sol or Clorox or both to clean up the cruiser and me.

I fantasized briefly with the idea of setting the cruiser on fire and having the Eden Volunteer Fire Department come, and just calling it a total loss.

Could I say they got into a pack of matches and set the car on fire? Would anyone believe I had been mugged by a band of baby raccoons?

I stood outside the cruiser and scrubbed away at my head, neck and pants. I heard distant chattering and scampering in the woods. It was the babies calling to each other, joining up and getting on with their lives and new freedom.

I stood up and took a closer look at the trees in front of me. Not my chosen location, but not bad. There was plenty of food for them here and they had each other. They were off to a good start, thanks to the kind folks at the Boy Scout camp.

I raised my near empty water jug in a toast to the masked vandals, drained the last drop into my mouth and laughed at myself.

Yes, I was a mess. And I had a good couple of hours of cruiser cleaning ahead of me, too. But as I rolled down all four windows and climbed into cruiser before driving away, I thought how lucky I was. I had a job that was never dull.

But that didn't mean I was an idiot.

From that day forward I made certain to carry a critter cage in the trunk of my cruiser just in case I might have to relocate some animal, no matter how young or how cute. I also learned to put a tarp under the cage to catch you know what and to place the cage and the tarp in an open trunk—not in the back seat—with a good selection of bungee cords for good measure, to control any future escape artists.

I vowed to take every possible precaution to keep cute and cuddly orphans as far away from me as possible. Not for their safety so much as mine.

They aren't called wild for nothing.

Warden's note: Never pick up or handle any wild animal of any age. Call your warden or a certified wildlife rehabilitator for help.

"I ran back to the front of the house, past my
neighbor and looked up and down the road.
Sure enough, there was the back end of a
bucking Mongo, galloping right up the yellow
center line, his cement block bouncing
along the pavement beside him."

MONGO

Vermont wardens don't punch a time clock. We are required to devote all the time necessary to do the job. Nights, weekends, and holidays—we are always on call. But we did have tacit approval to do some small-scale farming as long as it didn't interfere with our work.

I was young and had just moved to Eden with my wife, Jane, and our children. There was plenty of open ground at our new place for some animals and I wanted to try farming.

We had energy, but we didn't have a lot of money, so I started creating my own farm from whatever critters I could find on the cheap.

I promptly got a bunch of chickens and some pigs from locals who for the most part were overstocked and happy to sell at very reasonable prices. But I didn't have a "beefer"—a bull calf or young steer that I could fatten up on free grass over the summer and then have butchered in the fall to fill our freezer. That was something I really wanted.

I learned there was a regular cattle auction in nearby Morrisville and one day I swung in there to see if I could find myself a calf with the potential to grow fat fast and fill my freezer with tasty beef before the snow flew.

Sure enough, they had a yearling black and white bull of no particular parentage for sale. I got him at what I thought was a good price. He weighed about 250 pounds, was big-boned and looked like he would make some fine eating in the fall when he filled out on all that good grass down in back of my new home.

The guys at the auction helped pull and push him into the back of my pickup after I paid for him. He didn't appear to know a lot about leading. And when I got him home, he didn't want to come out of the back of the truck. I tugged on the improvised rope halter around his muzzle and behind his ears, but he wouldn't move. He was white eyed and dug in and almost sitting down on the rear window glass of the pick up, looking at me in terror.

At first I tried talking sweetly to him and pulling. When that didn't work I tried my warden voice. The calf wasn't impressed with my tender tones or my authoritative voice. I could not convince him to move. I was afraid if he sat down any more, his bony butt might smash my truck's rear view window and he could get stuck.

After five minutes of pleading and threats, I'd pretty much talked myself out. I shut up and sighed and let the pressure off the rope that was pinching his jaw shut. I guess that was the signal he had been waiting for.

The calf plunged forward, scrambling his hooves across the metal truck box. It sounded as if Santa's reindeers—all of them—spooked at once and were flying right at my head.

The calf didn't care that I was in the way. He was a split second from powering through me like a bovine linebacker. I jumped back and ducked beneath the tailgate. I looked up just in time to see a spotted pink and white belly fly over my head. His manure-encrusted tail smacked me in the side of the face.

The sisal rope went sizzling through my hand like it was attached to a big swordfish. When I straightened up, I was looking at a nasty rope burn across the palm of my right hand and the calf was loping about the front lawn in circles, wide eyed and foolish, dragging the lead line.

I didn't chase him. I figured he couldn't keep that dorky calf canter up for long. He'd get tired. He was staying away from the main road, so I gave him a minute or so to settle down. I took the time to spit on my palms to cool them down. But the thrill of having that calf almost take my head off made my salivary glands as dry as if I had spent a day in the Sahara.

As I stared at my hands trying to come up with a plan to catch him, I saw from the corner of my eye that the beast's head began to lower. I guess he recognized the green stuff beneath his feet was grass. He stopped trotting in circles and began to graze.

I took a couple deep breaths and began to formulate a plan as to how to deal with my future freezer filler. He might be scrawny, but he was sure strong.

I needed to get the calf to the pasture I had set up for him on the back side of the house, about 150 feet away.

A cutting horse would be nice. But we didn't have one and besides, I wasn't much of a rider and it would tear the heck out of the front lawn. Five guys with rodeo clown experience would be good too, but I didn't have them handy just now, either. My neighbors were wisely at work.

What to do?

He had grass. But what else motivates cattle? Grain? I hadn't bought any grain yet. But what was in the house that he might like?

I trotted inside the house and started rummaging through our kitchen cabinets. I hit upon the kids' cereal boxes and spied a box of Cheerios. That's grain, right? Maybe this bull calf would follow me if I walked in front of him with a box of Cheerios.

I hefted the box and shook it. Sounded like it was at least half full. I started for the door, then stopped and went to the kitchen sink and put the box down. I turned the faucet on cold and stuck my burning hands under the flow for a count of five. Wow, that cold water felt good. But I couldn't stay and enjoy it. I had a cattle round up to organize. I turned the faucet off, hiked up my pants, grabbed the cereal box and headed outside.

I found the calf not far from where I left him on the lawn. He was still happily eating grass. He didn't raise his head when I walked out of the house towards him, but I could clearly see him focus an eye on me. He was maybe 50 feet away.

With the Cheerios box in my left hand, my right palm still sore and smarting, I showed him the box and shook it a little so he could hear the crunchy rustle. I was hoping he had been raised on grain before and the Cheerio box shaking might make him want that treat.

He raised his head slightly.

I got within ten feet of him and walked past the halter rope lying in the grass. I decided my hands had been skinned enough. I wasn't going to pick up the rope at all. I wanted to convince the calf to come along with me, not try and force him. I had just learned the hard way that even at this tender age this animal was too darned strong for me to wrestle with alone.

The calf continued to graze, but shifted his behind towards me just in case he needed to make a run for it, I guess.

I held out the box of Cheerios to show it to him. Thinking back, I don't know if I expected him to read the label and believe that it was the breakfast of champions or what his dear mama used to feed him for breakfast or what all. All I know is shaking the box finally got his attention and he stopped chewing and his head came up a bit.

I stepped in and shook some of the Cheerios into my hand and let him sniff it. A big wet nose passed over the Cheerios and then his huge pink tongue came out and lapped them up. I froze and let him eat.

He took a step closer to me and I stepped back—one step closer to the back pasture.

I shook more cereal from the box into my hand and the calf appeared to have forgotten all about grazing. He took another step towards me. I began walking in reverse in earnest.

I was grinning at how well this was working, how smart I was and how easily trained the calf was. I only hoped I had enough cereal in the box to get us down into the backyard to his new fenced home.

I turned around and moved faster, the calf jogging beside me, stopping now and again to give him a handful when he butted me with his black and white head.

Luckily, the calf's appetite and the remaining cereal in the box kept pace with one another. I opened the gate to the pasture and he didn't hesitate to follow me in.

I poured the remainder of the box of Cheerios

on the ground and untied the rope from his neck as he munched. Then I scooted out of the gate, latched it and breathed a big sigh of relief.

I was a genius.

But this isn't the way the cowboys round up cattle in the movies, I thought. And then Blazing Saddles, one of my favorite movies came to mind.

I thought if Mel Brooks had seen how I drive cattle, he would have found a way to get that into the movie. I thought of the big, dumb, but good-hearted character in the movie, Mongo. And right then I knew I had the name for my beefer.

Mongo settled in pretty well for the first few days. He liked the big back pasture. The grass was green and there was plenty of it. And he could get a drink from the brook down by the woods.

At first he appeared content and willing to stay there by himself. However, within a few days that changed. I would find him grazing on the other side of the fence, on the back lawn, or worse, our front lawn bordering the busy highway.

I didn't want him hit by a car or knocking down my wife, Jane, or the kids. I spoke with a farmer friend who told me if you put some weight on a calf's neck, something for them to drag about, they are less likely to take off and break your fence.

I had some chimney block lying around—big rectangular concrete blocks with a hole in the middle for the tile liner—they weigh a good 40 or 50 pounds each. I figured one of them would slow a calf down if he had to drag it all day.

I boosted a block up into the bed of my pick up and drove down to the pasture gate. Then I borrowed the kids' Cheerios again and with a hank of rope I paid a visit to Mongo in the middle of the day inside the pasture. He came right up to greet me once he heard the sound of the Cheerios in the box. He seemed to like visiting with me now—too much, in fact.

I let myself inside the gate, moving like a matador in an attempt to dodge the bull running right into me. I knew it wasn't malicious, but Mongo just seemed to have no idea of the need for other creatures' personal space.

I poured a few cups of Cheerios in his feed dish and let him chase the little O's around with his nose and tongue while I quickly tied the rope to his neck and attached the other end to the heavy chimney block. Then I left the pasture and watched.

Mongo didn't seem at all upset about the neck weight when he raised his head. Maybe he thought the concrete block was his friend or something. I dunno.

His fence-busting antics stopped. It appeared the concrete block trick was a good one. I went to the local feed store and got Mongo a salt lick and some grain, thinking it would speed his weight gain.

Every morning I'd walk down from the house to give Mongo a scoop of grain and a bucket of fresh water—just in case the brook was muddy or drying up.

Mongo got so he loved to see me coming. He would come running towards me, cement block bouncing along merrily beside him. I had to get inside the gate to water and grain him. As he grew, it was a challenge for me to not get run over.

He seemed to think he was a lap dog in a bull's body.

I was stepped on, head butted, swatted

across the face with a manure-filled tail, and continually body slammed by him. Grabbing onto the rope around his neck was not a solution. He was all muscle and sinew under that polka dot hide.

He would throw his head up and yank me off my feet trying to get to the grain. One of his favorite tricks was to use my body as a scratching post.

Hold on tight to the rope and my arms could be yanked out of the sockets. Let him go and I had no control at all. I considered bringing in a cape like a matador to get around him.

Mongo was growing up, not out. He seemed to be getting stronger, but not fatter. I loosened the rope around his neck, but I kept the cement block on the other end tied fast. Adjusting the rope was its own personal challenge, because he loved to rub on me.

I would leave the pasture covered in calf snot and hair with my back aching. Sometimes I got stepped on too. I was pretty sure he busted at least one of my toes.

The bigger Mongo got, the smaller the cement block looked.

And it wasn't long before the concrete block

didn't seem to deter him at all from busting the fence.

I was spending a lot of time fixing fence and a substantial amount of money on Cheerios—which was my secret weapon for coaxing him back inside the pasture after he broke out—and my chiropractor was doing well, too. The kids learned to like other cereal for breakfast. If there was just one box of Cheerios in the cabinet, Jane had to give the kids the bad news that it was reserved for Mongo.

All of this was kind of cute when Mongo only weighed 250 lbs, but at 600 plus pounds his pushing and rubbing and running at me was getting dangerous. He was behaving like a bull.

Sometimes his head would be down as he came running at me for his breakfast. I guess he wanted to play.

I discouraged this behavior with a light kick in the nose with my rubber barn boot on the mornings he came charging at me for his grain. It was that or Mongo would run me over.

So that became our routine. Mongo would be down in the lower pasture grazing on grass, but looking up at the house and watching it carefully for any sign of movement. The sound of a door slamming or a human outside meant breakfast to Mongo.

When he saw me coming around the corner of the house, he would run hell bent for leather towards the fence, sometimes silent, sometimes bellering. The challenge was for me to get into the pasture to his feed bowl and water trough before he got to the gate. If I was too slow, he might bust right through the fencing to get to me.

If he beat me up the hill and broke through the fence before I got inside the gate to feed him, I'd then have a good half hour of fixing fence ahead of me.

And it wasn't just me that Mongo associated with food or someone to run at. Mongo started racing up the hill when any vehicle pulled in the driveway. Depending on his mood, he would bust the fence and charge them.

I began to discourage friends and colleagues from visiting. I would meet them in town.

We had to give up the use of our backyard because Mongo might bust through and slobber all over us and send the kids screaming back into the house.

Mongo even learned to watch the windows.

Maybe he figured if we were going to stare into
his house, he was going to keep an eye on ours
as well. I don't know. But I do know if he saw
someone inside the house it would stir him
up and start him mooing. So, we pulled the
curtains tight on the back of the house, which
included the kitchen, and did our best to not let
him see us.

Jane and I agreed neither she nor any of the
kids should spend time in the backyard because
Mongo might just come charging up and
through the fence looking for company.

About the only thing Mongo was afraid of
was the lawn mower. Maybe it hurt his ears.
Maybe it was the fact it sprayed grass—his
food—all over. I was just grateful I found
something that would keep him from coming
after me. If I wanted to do some work outdoors,
I learned to run the mower first. That sent him
running to the back of the pasture and away
from me.

Our world was getting very small. The kids
could not play out back. We had to sneak
in and out of our house by parking out front
because we did not want Mongo to see us. We
had to keep the curtains pulled on the back of

the house for fear Mongo would spot us and start bellering.

I told Jane and the kids that come winter, when Mongo was in the freezer and we had roasts, stews, chops and hamburgers to eat, we would forget about this momentary inconvenience.

I think I was trying to convince myself. I continued to feed and water Mongo and monitor his growth in between answering countless calls and department duties. Raising this beefer was not supposed to be this much work.

It was a bright September morning and I was sitting in the living room, discussing assignments for the week with one of my deputies. He had parked out front so Mongo would not spot him. I heard pounding on my front door.

I opened the door to find my neighbor.

"Eric, is that your bull running up Route 100?" he asked breathlessly.

I ran to the kitchen, pulled open the curtains and looked out over the pasture. Sure enough, there wasn't a sign of Mongo. My guess was Mongo thought I was a few minutes late with his breakfast and that had prompted him to bust out and come looking for me. He kept me on a short leash.

I ran back to the front of the house, past my neighbor and looked up and down the road. Sure enough, there was the back end of a bucking Mongo, galloping right up the yellow center line, his cement block bouncing along the pavement beside him.

A car approached the calf and swerved. I realized now how huge Mongo had become. His head towered over the car roof. The block he was towing looked like he had dropped his pocket watch and chain.

Fortunately, the morning commute was over. I turned to my neighbor and said, "Yeah, that's my bull all right. Thanks."

Then I surprised my neighbor and deputy by running back into the kitchen. But there was a method to my madness. I grabbed the box of Cheerios from the kitchen cabinet, ran back through the living room and out the front door. I ran against traffic and as cars passed me, they looked more than a little puzzled. I guess it's not every day you see a game warden running down a road, yelling, "MONGO," and waving a box of Cheerios.

Did they think I was chasing my kids' school bus wanting them to eat a healthy breakfast?

I topped a small rise and there was Mongo, nibbling grass in a ditch. The few cars on the road headed towards him were wisely slowing down and driving wide past him.

Mongo looked up when he heard my voice and the familiar sound of the Cheerios in the box. He stopped grazing, lifted his front feet out of the ditch and strolled on up to me and nuzzled the box, his big red tongue giving it a lick. Then he butted me with his head, rocking me back on my heels.

Mongo was not a bovine to hold a grudge. He wasn't being mean. It was his way of saying, "I missed you and I'm hungry."

I looked at the rope around his neck and then down at the cement block in the grass. His anchor was a shadow of its former self.

I gave Mongo a handful of Cheerios, spoke to him calmly, patted him on the neck, then looked both ways, and started trotting down the road towards home, shaking the box and calling to him. He knew the routine well and it didn't take much urging to get him to follow me. Mongo began trotting a pace or two behind me back to the house.

I was a cowboy with an invisible cow pony beneath me, holding the cereal box in my left hand and occasionally slapping my thigh with my right hand to keep the bull's attention on me.

To keep the steer focused, every once in awhile I would dump a handful of Cheerios from the box into my right hand and let him lick them up as we jogged along together.

The concrete block, now sized more like a brick, bounced erratically along behind the two of us, occasionally shooting up little flinty sparks as the block struck stones in the road.

Tourists pulled over and grabbed their cameras. A few locals drove past and grinned. Maybe they thought they were witnessing some sort of Northeast Kingdom warden-bovine agility training.

I got several big smiles, waves and thumbs up from folks I knew. I held my head up and pretended Mongo was the best trained bull in the county and we were getting ready for the fair.

As I rounded the corner leading to my front yard, I spied my deputy still dutifully waiting for me. I yelled for him to go around back and open the pasture gate.

I didn't dare stop for fear Mongo would run right over the top of me.

With the pasture gate open, I dove inside, poured the rest of the Cheerios in Mongo's grain bucket and stepped aside with a lowered shoulder and spun like a matador. I circled around his big hairy rump and pulled the gate shut behind me. Then I breathed a big sigh of relief.

My deputy finally spoke. "Nice move," he said. He would go far.

As for me, that jog down the highway had cleared my head. I was looking at Mongo in a whole new light as he stood there calmly swishing his tail and eating the kids' Cheerios—again.

I sighed and said, "Thanks for your help. This beef-raising enterprise isn't quite going as I'd planned. Go on in and get yourself another cup of coffee. I've got to fix the fence and give him his grain. Will only take a minute."

I grabbed some wire and my pliers and went to work, looking at Mongo and thinking, "Was it worth another two or three months of me being bumped, stepped on, body slammed and bruised, my kids unable to play outside, my wife unable to open the curtains, to get another 25 pounds of steaks and hamburger in the freezer? To live like this?"

I walked inside and the phone rang.

A truck in a neighboring town had hit a moose. It was dead. Would I come over and remove it? I took it as an answer from above. I looked at the calendar on my desk. The regular monthly cattle auction was two days away.

Another sign.

I didn't hesitate. I phoned a friend with a horse trailer and arranged for him to take Mongo back to the auction house first thing in the morning. My deputy sipped his coffee and didn't say a word.

Did I tell you how smart this guy was?

When I hung up the phone the third time, I said, "Let's go get a moose."

It was a nice young cow, good weight, fattened up on summer feed. She'd make a lot of good eating. We winched her into the back of my pick up and drove the carcass 25 miles to a meat processor. I called my boss and asked if I could buy the moose meat. He gave his approval.

My buddy came over bright and early the next morning with his horse trailer and parked it in our driveway.

He lowered the gate and I walked in and spread a trail of grain inside with a big pile at the far end. Then I walked down to the pasture with the box of Cheerios and a knife. I swung the gate wide open and cut the rope from Mongo's neck with one hand while I gave him a handful of Cheerios with the other. He licked up the cereal and rubbed on me, rocking me back on my heels for the last time.

I shook the box and walked through the back yard towards the trailer. Mongo pranced beside me like a circus pony. He paused at the trailer ramp, but with a little more coaxing and the Cheerios, he loaded without incident.

My horse friend was some impressed with my bull handling skills.

"Wow, Eric. You really have that animal trained," he said. "If he only knew," I thought to myself.

I gave Mongo a pat on the rump along with my best wishes for a long and happy life—just not at my house—and I gave my friend the remainder of the box of Cheerios and grain to help him unload Mongo. My buddy closed up the trailer gate and down the road they went.

I got a check a week later in the mail from the auction house.

I had added up my expenses: purchase price, grain, the multiple boxes of Cheerios and the trailer fee to get him back to the auction house. On paper it didn't look too bad. I could almost argue I about broke even.

But the hassle?

I vowed to never raise a beefer again. Leave it to the experts. Pay the price for a roast or steak and tip your hat to the farmers and ranchers who raise them. Don't complain. It is hard, dirty and dangerous work.

I used the money selling Mongo to buy the cow moose from the Department, have the meat cut up, wrapped and frozen. Instead of beef we ate moose all winter. Delicious.

Best of all, with Mongo gone, we threw open the curtains and let the sun shine in. Our reign of beefer terror was over. The kids played in the backyard and had friends over. I stopped walking like a beat up cowboy. My mashed toes and sore back began to heal.

Jane and I threw a party and invited friends over. We put moose burgers and moose steaks on the grill out back.

Of course, the guys couldn't help but notice the big fenced pasture with the couple of nice shade trees and that sweet little brook down below.

More than one of them said, "Hey, Eric, you ever think about raising your own beef? You've got a perfect spot here."

I shuddered whenever the topic came up.

"Oh, Jane and the kids and I like moose a lot better. Healthier for you too," I'd say.

"Ain't that the truth," I'd chuckle to myself. "My sore back, my knees, my mashed toes are just about healed. Yup, I'm sure a lot healthier since I sold my one bull herd."

Then I would immediately change the subject.

"Hey, how those Red Sox? Think they'll make the play offs?"

"We were trading off for about the fifth time
when we both spied a couple guys fishing off a
bridge atop the Clyde Dam. They were maybe
100 yards from us. The anglers smiled and
waved. One had his pole in the water.
The other was baiting his hook
and preparing to cast. Bob said
from the underside of the canoe,
"Eric, you see those guys?"

CLYDE RIVER RACE

How to get enough quality time on Vermont's pristine rivers when I had a job to do?

My solution was to combine work with pleasure. And I convinced the Department that I could do very effective enforcement work from my canoe. It was a little self-serving, but it worked.

In fact, I'd convinced a warden friend named Bob Baird to join me in my innovative enforcement efforts—by sitting in the bow.

I didn't have to twist Bob's arm. He loves being on the water, too.

Better two wardens working together traveling white water or tackling the occasional angler with attitude, I figured. It also didn't hurt that Bob has exceptionally powerful shoulders and arms and I wouldn't have to work so hard.

As canoeing partners, Bob was the motor and

I was the brain—or that's the way I saw it
anyway. Bob would likely tell you that he was
the motor and the brains and all I did from my
position in the stern was watch the scenery
go by or nap. He liked to joke that I only
put a paddle in the water when disaster was
imminent.

And I must admit there might have been a
moment or two in our numerous outings when
I was a little slow in picking up my paddle.
Luckily Bob also has good lungs. His screaming
from the bow when we were about to be
smashed to pieces on one boulder or another
almost always woke me up.

For whatever reason, Bob put up with me as a
canoeing partner. We patrolled the backwaters
regularly together in northern Vermont and
called it work.

We'd leave one cruiser at our end point and then
drive up the road along the stream as far as we
could in the other, unload our canoe, throw on
our life vests, get in and go. Wherever there
were anglers in the water or along the river
bank, we stopped and checked them out.

Over the years I've learned that anglers with a
guilty conscience have trouble focusing on their
fishing. They spend a lot of time looking over

their shoulder, consciously or unconsciously looking to the riverbanks for a law officer that might bust them.

Brook and river anglers never figure on a warden canoeing down on top of them to check their license and creel. A warden can cover miles of water in just a few hours in a canoe or kayak. You can check a lot of licenses and creels in a day this way. It was much more effective than being on foot.

After a couple years of regular patrols by canoe and some white water fun runs in our free time, I began to think that Bob and I ought to enter a race somewhere together. I began to look for opportunities close to home.

I spied a poster announcing the annual spring Clyde River Canoe Race. The race was about 15 miles long, with a half mile portage in the middle adding to the challenge. We would start in Salem and end in Newport at the town park on the shores of Lake Memphremagog. The lake borders southern Quebec.

The Clyde was held during the spring runoff, and depending on the amount of winter snow in the mountains and spring rains, it could create a wild ride for participants. Locals and tourists alike enjoyed watching the cold water dunking that was the fate of many brave—some would say foolish—competitors.

Bob and I had canoed a lot of the race route before as part of our work patrols. So we knew where the big water hazards were. We were both in very good physical condition from snowshoeing and cross country skiing Vermont's woods throughout the winter, enforcing the law.

All in all, I thought we had a pretty good chance at winning or at least not embarrassing ourselves.

I was prepared to rattle off all the above reasons and more to Bob in case he didn't want to enter. But I quickly found I didn't need to convince him at all. Bob is as competitive as I am. As soon as I mentioned that I saw the river race poster, Bob said, "We ought to enter!"

We let our supervisors know as a courtesy and everyone agreed it was best if we were out of uniform that day. Most of the local folks would know who we were anyhow but better to keep it low key. This was not a Department function. We were just happy to have the green light to enter the race.

The Clyde starts with a lineup on Salem Lake where all the two-man teams jostle for position. The trick is to get a good spot while not smacking a paddle into a competitor's face, ramming someone else's canoe or dumping other canoe racers into the frigid waters. That stuff happens, and is part of the excitement, but not on purpose.

Race day was frosty, the sun bright, and the water icy cold. At the starting line, we were in the middle of a pack of about 25 two man teams. It was tough to get any kind of line up, as the water was just blasting white and frothy. When the gun sounded, Bob and I got off to a good start, but our progress was slowed considerably when two attorney friends capsized less than 200 feet from the starting line, right in front of our canoe.

Bob pushed hard aft so as not to drift over their heads and I did my best to follow him.

I dished my paddle deep in the roiled water to try and slow us down, turn our canoe and offer the gasping swimmers a hand.

Both were wearing life vests. There wasn't a lot of danger of them drowning. But they could be run over or slammed in the head by a competing canoe.

All around us were dipping, tipping, bouncing,

slamming, jamming canoes and screaming paddlers trying to get past this traffic jam.

Bob and I were big on good intentions, but short on water rescue skills. We drifted cross current and I accidentally slammed one friend in the head with a paddle and we rode over the top of our other pal. If we kept this up we might just kill them.

One of the pair waved for us to go away. They decided to take their chances in the icy current rather than have me beat them unconscious.

We gave up, straightened up the canoe and rejoined the race. But looking in front of us, I saw we had lost some serious time trying to be helpful. We were way back of the pack. Bob and I gritted our teeth and dug in. Maybe we could make up our lost time in the portage, where we both figured many competitors would be undone.

More than a simple white water race, the Clyde demands that competitors portage around Clyde Pond a half mile or so. The pond is a popular fishing hole created by the Clyde Dam and Citizen's Utilities Number 11 Dam.

The portage required having the wind, leg and shoulder strength to pick up the canoe, paddles and gear and dash through mud, tree roots, snow and icy patches up and down hills.

I figured this piece would slow down many of these weekend warriors and give us a chance to make up for lost time.

We managed to arrive at the Clyde Pond shore upright, a little wet, but ready to carry. We quickly pulled the canoe on shore.

Our technique was a little different than most teams. Just one of us would carry the canoe at a time, trading back and forth. The other guy trots along giving directions if necessary and when it is his turn, ducks under while the other fellow scoots out.

I think this is more efficient than two guys trying to coordinate their steps like a centipede.

Our canoe was aluminum and weighed about 70 pounds. The trick is to lift and flip the canoe over your head and put the center thwart, with a yoke built right into it, on top of your shoulders. Then you lean the prow back a bit, so the stern drops and you can see the trail as you trot on. With your fingers tight to the gunwales to steady the craft, you can make good time.

Or so I hoped.

We were about to find out.

Bob grabbed our paddles and gear while I hoisted the canoe to my shoulders and set off at a trot.

Each of us carried the canoe about 200 yards Then the other would dip underneath the gunwales, place the yoke on his shoulders, let the other man slide out and run ahead.

We were trading off for about the fifth time when we both spied a couple guys fishing off a bridge atop the Clyde Dam. They were maybe 100 yards from us. The anglers smiled and waved. One had his pole in the water. The other was baiting his hook and preparing to cast.

Bob shouted out from the underside of the canoe, "Eric, do you see those guys?"

I said, "Yeah," and ducked my head between the thwarts, grabbed tight onto the gunwales and kept running.

As I trotted with the canoe on top of my shoulders, I knew Bob and I were thinking the same thing. Trout season had opened a week earlier, but that was stream fishing. Bass season was a month away. So, what species were these guys trying to catch that were in season?

"Later," I said to myself and I turned my attention back to the race.

We were making really good time. Bob and I passed another half dozen teams struggling with their two man canoe carry technique.

We managed to hit the water at the end of the portage like two otters sharing a surfboard. No fumbling. We were in and away and back on the water headed to the finish line—still behind the leaders, but gaining on 'em.

As we got out into the broad water of Lake Memphramagog, headed for the finish line, we saw we were in the top third of the pack.

We still had a chance to win it.

Bob began counting out loud so that our strokes would be in unison. It was time for turbo. All our work sessions began to pay off. We paddled furiously towards the finish line a few miles ahead.

The wind was with us, the waves were less than a foot. It was still cold enough to chap your lips and freeze your molars, but we were loving it. We were flying across the water as if we were Canadian voyageurs 200 years earlier. We passed three canoes as if we were Secretariat.

As we approached the finish line, a small crowd was hooting and hollering and clapping their mittened hands. We bore down harder but just could not catch the one team left in front of us.

We finished second.

Bob and I were grinning ear to ear as we beached our canoe at the edge of the beautiful Newport green to accept congratulatory slaps on the back from our friends and family.

After catching our breath and gulping some hot tea from a thermos offered to us, we walked over to congratulate the first place finishers.

We had just finished shaking their hands when a friend who had followed the action walked up to Bob and me to ask if we had seen the guys on the bridge holding up the bass.

What? Bass season wasn't set to open for another month. Nope, we'd seen the guys fishing, we said, but we didn't see them catch anything.

Bob and I looked at each other and sighed. We knew what we had to do. I felt for my truck keys in my pocket, pulled them out and held them up. Bob grinned and said, "Let's go."

We excused ourselves, trotted over to my truck

and sped off. I had parked my truck near the finish line very early that morning and we had taken Bob's vehicle down to the race starting point.

Sure enough, there were the two fellows, still fishing off the dam bridge. We climbed up the bank and started a conversation with them.

"Having any luck?" Bob asked them.

"Yeah, got two nice bass," one young fellow said proudly, holding up his stringer. It was pretty clear the pair didn't realize bass season wouldn't open for another month.

"You guys were in that race, right?" the other fellow said. "Wow, you two can really make a canoe fly," he added.

Bob and I thanked them for the compliment and then "rolled our gold" as we like to say. In as nice a way as we could, we gave them the bad news that they wouldn't be eating bass that night.

They were genuinely surprised. Not just that we were wardens, but that they were doing something illegal.

Each of them showed us valid Vermont fishing

licenses. They were visiting Vermont from Canada and had purchased their licenses the day before. The problem was they hadn't picked up and read the booklet that lets anglers and hunters know when Vermont's fishing and hunting seasons open and close.

After a quick lesson on that subject we issued the men warnings, seized their fish and told them they were done for the day. They were contrite and thanked us for not throwing the book at them.

Then Bob and I drove back to the park. We pulled into the parking lot just in time for the awards ceremony.

We were pretty happy to collect the trophy for second place.

What Bob and I didn't know until a few days later was that our little disappearing act had raised a lot of eyebrows and started the local rumor mill churning big time.

Within 72 hours the local diners and bars were rife with rumors about two undercover cops who competed in the Clyde River Race, busted a couple major fugitives along the way and still managed to finish second. Depending on who was telling the story, the guys the cops nabbed were drug runners, smugglers or illegal aliens.

And some people claimed the Clyde River Race itself was just an excuse for these kind of international undercover operations.

Wow. When the stories got back to us, Bob and I had some good laughs.

Like I said, our backwater canoe patrols were good for wildlife, good for the department and good for law enforcement in general.

Bob and I have the trophy to prove it.

"Mark yipped, threw himself forward and with a
big squeal of hunting dog lust, he yanked me face
down onto the forest floor duff, snapped
the clothesline lead and took off after
that doe without me."

HUNT 'ER UP

It was a cold November night and I was warm in bed next to my wife when I got the call from the state police dispatcher.

A driver navigating a winding back road outside of Hardwick had hit a deer. It was my friend, Warden John K's territory, but John was tied up with another call.

As the dispatcher explained it, the car was pretty busted up and there was hair and blood in the grill. The car needed towing, but the deer had taken off. The trooper figured the deer could not have gone far and he had to wait for the tow truck operator. Would I come and find the deer and put it out of its misery?

Now normally, I would not be excited about such a call. But I had spent a lot of time that summer working with my young Golden Retriever mix, Mark, preparing him for just such an opportunity.

I gave my sleeping wife a peck on the cheek and jumped outta bed. I was dressed and in the truck with Mark wagging his tail beside me in less than five minutes. Mark loved to ride. All you had to do was open his kennel and head to the truck. He was inside in a flash.

I had been inspired to recruit Mark in this effort by one of our top wardens from southern Vermont. He had been regaling us with the exceptional deer tracking skills of his black lab. The way my colleague went on, all he had to do was open the truck door, and the dog did the rest.

He said he could put that lab of his on a wounded deer track, say, "Hunt 'er up," and with a wink, thumbs up and bold leap into the pucker brush, in no time at all that lab would find the deer.

The dog would text message the downed deer's location using GPS. Once the dog had sent up a flare because cell phone coverage was spotty in the area. He claimed his canine never missed.

This guy tended to exaggerate a little. But we all got the point that his wonder puppy saved him a lot of time fumbling around in the woods doing the old tracker trick of looking for blood and tracks as we were trained to do.

I had to admit, I was a little envious. Having a dog's nose and eyes do the job for you seemed like a much better idea than a man with a flashlight bent over staring at leaf litter.

Mark had been given to me as a gangly golden-haired pup about eighteen months earlier. He wasn't a purebred, but he was a handsome boy. I love fall bird hunting and I was always in the market for another good bird dog.

But as Mark grew from a puppy to hunting dog maturity, it became apparent that he had a little problem with focus. In terms of hunting interests, he was a generalist, not a specialist. Mark would chase just about anything if he was in the mood. On a bird hunt he might give it a go, but if a deer popped up, his interest in birds flew away. To Mark, bigger was better. So, his quarry of choice became deer.

I tried hard for a long time to get Mark to focus only on birds. We had long discussions about his heritage and breeding. I showed him pictures of birds and brought him downed birds so he could smell and fawn over them.

I took him out with friends and their well trained dogs. I worked him alongside other retrievers to try to convince him that he was born to flush birds and birds alone.

But time and again Mark made it clear to me that he preferred fur to feathers. It got so bad the other guys didn't want me to take Mark out with us on hunts, for fear he would start their dogs chasing deer as well. I had to admit he might.

It is against the law in Vermont for dogs to chase deer except under very limited circumstances, such as working to locate wounded deer under the control of a game warden.

So, unable to break Mark of his fondness for chasing deer after more than a year of trying, I decided to take a negative and turn it into a positive. I saw no reason Mark couldn't be just as successful as my bragging colleague's black lab cousin and become useful as a deer dog and help me do my job.

We worked at it together, with me keeping Mark on a short leash, never letting him run unsupervised in deer country. He had basic commands down. After some weeks of proven success at finding deer scent, I was confident Mark was ready for prime time. That's why I was almost giddy to be getting out of bed at 1 am.

The trooper was still at the scene when I got there, waiting for the tow truck to arrive. The female driver of the car was there too, shook up,

but not hurt. She was waiting for her husband
to come and give her a ride home.

I rolled down my window to introduce myself.
The trooper looked at me, then saw the gold
head and shoulders standing on my lap, poking
his head out of the truck window.

"A little early in the day to go duck hunting, isn't
it, Warden?" he joked. I guess he was expecting
some sort of hound dog to handle this job.

I took the joke well, chuckled and responded
with pride, "This is Mark. He's a deer tracking
dog. Saves me a lot of work."

"Oh," the trooper said, sounding impressed
with the concept. I pushed Mark off my lap and
pawed around the bench seat beside me for his
lead line.

The trooper stepped back and waited for us to
get out. But I wasn't about to get out of the cab
until I had the dog's collar firmly snapped to his
lead. Mark was an eager dog. He might jump
out and decide to go find the deer without me.

There was every manner of warden supplies
in the front seat next to me—shotgun shells,
three or four pairs of binoculars and scopes
and their cases, rain coats and a tarp, boots

and paperwork of all kinds, but no lead rope. Suddenly it dawned on me that in my haste, I had left it back at the house.

What to use?

I had so wanted to appear well organized, but I wasn't. So, I said "Excuse me," and turned my back on the trooper, flicked the cab dome light on and desperately began digging through an avalanche of loose papers, file folders, boxes of shotgun shells, muddy coats and a good three-month collection of other warden stuff. Finally, I tried the second tier of storage—the floor on the passenger seat. And there my hand hit upon a tangle of frayed and knotted cotton clothesline. I'd used it to tie down a canoe on my trailer a few weeks earlier. It would have to do.

I sat up and looped and knotted one end of the well used rope to Mark's collar. I wrapped the other end around my hand, grabbed my flashlight and hat, and opened the truck cab door. Mark leaped to the ground, spinning like a top until he landed both front paws on the trooper's crisp-pressed green trousers.

I tried to pull the dog back before he climbed all over my fellow officer, but the lead rope spooled out of my hand. Apparently the trooper expected to have some police academy-

trained German shepherd step out of a cruiser
and sit down politely, waiting for a command.
That would have been impressive. But that
wasn't Mark. He was short on manners,
especially when excited. And he was excited
most of the time.

Before I could shut the truck door, Mark was
standing on his hind legs, jumping on my
colleague's shiny black boots, trying to lick the
officer's face. I saw dog drool dripping down
onto the trooper's knees.

I reeled in the line as quick as I could and
yanked Mark back towards me. On the way
back to earth, Mark got in a couple quick
trooper hand licks, then he hit the ground on
all fours and began spinning in circles.

"Friendly," the trooper said, with less enthusiasm
in his voice. He was brushing paw prints off his
shirt and trousers, out of reach of Mark's paws.
He stepped back like a maitre d' in an expensive
French restaurant and with a grand gesture
swing of his right arm said, "This way." He led
us past the car with the smashed grill and leaky
radiator at the side of the road.

Mark's nose went up in the air as we got closer
to the disabled vehicle. He was sucking up
scent like a car wash vacuum cleaner stealing all

your loose change. I let him have a good sniff of the front of the car, then we checked out the side of the road.

"I figure the deer went in about here," the trooper said. Mark agreed. He was so excited he started to whine. I nodded to the officer and said with quiet confidence, "Thanks. That should do it."

I turned to Mark and for dramatic effect said, "Ready, Boy?" Mark was shivering and squealing now with anticipation and I was losing circulation in my hand as he tugged on the rope.

I was grinning inside knowing that all my training and hard work with this dog would shine here at last. I was prepared to dazzle the audience with Mark's skills and my incredible handling of him.

"Hunt 'er up!" I said with enough volume for the trooper and lady driver to hear.

I turned on my flashlight beam and stepped off the road edge towards the woods. I wanted the taxpayer to see she was getting her money's worth in this emergency. In her hour of need in the dark of night on a back road on a bitter cold night, this lady was getting a trooper, a warden and a highly-trained deer dog too.

I let a couple feet of clothesline roll off my palm so Mark could move into the woods easily and not choke himself to death.

Mark had apparently been waiting for just that moment. He reared up like a stallion, pawed the air briefly and threw himself forward, taking me head first with him.

One second I was standing at the roadside scanning the woods with my flashlight beam and looking like a top notch dog handler, when boom, Mark yanked me off my feet.

My flashlight beam swung down at my boots, then up to the stars. Mark was 85 pounds of wild hunting dog and tired of waiting. I had all I could do not to fall flat on my face into the ditch.

I had already made a mental note to work on the leashing part inside the truck cab the next time. Now I made another note to work on our departure.

Oh well, at least we were both smiling when we left the roadside stage.

Mark and I plunged into the woods, crashing through trees. He was definitely on the scent. His nose was at ground level and he was moving so fast I couldn't see anything but shadows. I had to shut my eyes so as not to get them poked out by tree branches.

I crouched down low to get beneath the bigger branches. I was walking like Groucho Marx—leaning back to hold the dog with one hand—shining the light ahead with the other, picking my feet way up high in front of me so as not to trip over rocks, roots and stumps.

I figured the closer to the ground I walked, the less likely I was to clobber myself in the forehead with a stout three or four inch branch. I could not pull back hard on the cotton rope for fear it might break and I would lose Mark. I had to try and stay with him.

My face was whipped and stung by branches and twigs. I found myself spitting out balsam needles. I desperately wanted to yank the dog back and tell him to slow down. But I didn't want the folks at the roadway to hear me and think I wasn't in control.

For all of his enthusiasm, Mark was a sensitive dog and he was clearly on the trail of a deer. He wouldn't be so excited otherwise. But by the time I was 50 feet into the woods, I was grinding my teeth and hissing, "Mark, slow down!

Eas-eeee. Slow the blue blazes down!"

Despite my pleadings, I didn't experience any noticeable change of pace from Mark. He kept plowing ahead in the darkness, his breathing growing more frantic and hoarse. He might be choking himself to death, but he wasn't going to stop until he found that deer or died doing it.

Then, about 100 yards into the chase, Mark stopped dead in his tracks and I didn't. I stumbled hard forward, tripped over some brush and caught myself just before my nose hit the leaf litter.

Slowly, I righted myself and swung my light in the direction he was staring. And there she was. Two eyes about five feet above the forest floor, maybe fifty feet straight ahead of us. A deer. I looked more closely and saw blood on her shoulder. She had to be the deer the driver had hit. She didn't look wobbly. I was a lot wobblier than the doe.

Mark had done his job—at warp speed—and found the deer. So what if I was spitting up pine needles and almost split my skull plowing into trees? Mark had found the deer! But I couldn't congratulate him just yet.

It was time to put this poor doe out of her misery. To do that I had to get my revolver out of the holster. I slowly reached across the front of my body to pass the flashlight from my right hand to my left so I could use my right hand to reach my weapon. My left hand was bound tight by the final few wraps of knotted up clothesline.

Mark was frozen in place staring at the deer, which was doing the same frozen animal act back at him. No one was making a sound. If the dog and the deer would just hold still a few seconds longer, it would all be over. The doe would be out of her misery and Mark and I would be heroes.

Wardens are taught that if you hold the flashlight on the top of your head, the edge of the beam will illuminate the gun sights and the target together. You can get off a pretty accurate shot this way. It looks a little silly in practice, but it works well. And besides, nobody makes fun of the guy with the gun.

In retrospect, I don't think the maneuver I was taught was designed to be used when working with a deer crazed dog on rotted clothesline in the middle of the woods at 2 am.

I got my revolver out, raised the light above my head and was just about to squeeze off a shot when the doe blinked.

Holding still was not one of Mark's strong points.

He wasn't a pointer. He was a retriever. He wanted to bring me the deer, not stand still and stare at it.

Mark yipped and threw himself forward. With a big squeal of hunting dog lust, he jumped up and twisted in the air like a 600 pound marlin.

I was thrown forward, tripped on a tree root and went flying through the air.

My flashlight was knocked out of my hand and went skittering across the forest floor. I flew a good eight feet or more thanks to Mark's mighty tow. I landed spread eagle, face down in the leaf litter, my right hand still holding tight to my revolver.

No shots fired. But dog long gone. Mark had broken the cotton lead.

I climbed to my knees, spit out a couple teaspoons of forest floor, holstered my revolver and unwrapped what was left of the clothesline from my left hand. I stood up and dashed through the shadows to retrieve my still shining flashlight. It had landed a good 10 feet away.

I picked it up and went running after my dog.

There was no way I could even pretend to be

cool and collected now. I needed to call Mark in before he chased the doe to the next county or worse, caught her.

"MARK! MARK! COME!" I yelled. All around me was the crashing and banging of deer, dog and me in the dark.

"MARK, COME!"

More deer and dog crashing through the woods, followed by me shining the light in wide arcs, side to side, and calling again and again. I tried to be methodical. I trotted about 50 paces, stopped, listened and called hoping to get Mark to come in to me. But all I heard was yipping and branches breaking.

It is true what they say about the night—how your hearing becomes more acute.

I know this, because, while I thought I was a pretty good distance into the woods from where the deer was struck by the car, whenever I stopped to listen and try to figure out which way Mark was running, I began to hear laughter.

It started out as snickers and guffaws, but the more I stopped to call to Mark, the louder the laughter became.

First, it was just one man laughing, but as Mark crashed around in the woods and I kept calling to him, a second voice was also heard laughing—that of a woman.

It eventually turned into pee-your-pants hilarity back there on the road—a midnight comedy show and I was the main act.

I wasn't laughing.

If I could have seen the dog, I might have just dropped him then and there and left him in the woods. But Mark and his new best friend, the doe, were too fast. They were running wide circles around me in the dark for better than a half hour.

It finally struck me then that any deer that could run that fast for that long could not be hurt too bad. No need to track her down and put her out of her misery.

It was me who was in misery now—how the heck was I going to get Mark back and how was I ever going to live this down?

I knew the area and I knew deer. I figured the doe would eventually lead Mark to a stream about 100 yards in front of us to try and hide her scent. I headed that way. I had to go somewhere and I sure as heck wasn't about to go back to my truck until the trooper and the lady driver and the tow truck operator were all gone. I walked away from the road and down to the brook. If nothing else, I wouldn't be able to hear the folks at the roadside laughing.

Maybe the cold water in the brook brought Mark back to his senses. Maybe he just got tired of running. Maybe he and the deer decided to shake hands and call it a night, I don't know. But about an hour after he broke the lead line, Mark found me. His head was down, his tongue was about dragging on the forest floor. His tail sawed the dark slowly side to side. He was soaking wet, panting and grinning ear to ear.

Mark crouched low coming into me. I took it as a sincere doggie apology on his part. I guessed he had gone down to the brook and jumped in to cool off.

I had cooled off a bit myself. My face was still stinging from tree whips slapping me the first 10 minutes of our run, my knees were a little sore from landing on rocks back there when he yanked me down. But the facts were Mark had found the deer trail, tracked the deer and even done his best to point it out. He did a good job for his first time. It wasn't Mark's fault the deer blinked and the rotten rope snapped.

I had the remainder of clothesline lead in my hand, but there was no need to put a lead on Mark now. He was spent.

So, I said, "Good dog. Let's go home," and bent down to give his ears a rub while he licked my hands. Mark followed behind me quietly all the way back to the highway. We came out of the woods a few hundred yards above the accident scene.

There, I tied the ratty piece of line I still had with me to his collar, just in case vehicles approached. We walked in silence along the roadway—both of us with our tails dragging—to my truck. We'd been in the woods about two hours. In another hour or so it would be dawn.

Back at my truck, the trooper, the driver and the deer-damaged car were all gone. I was glad for that. Mark and I climbed up into the truck cab. He immediately curled up on the seat beside me and closed his eyes.

I was about to fire up the truck, when I saw headlights coming towards us. The operator pulled up beside me. It was John. He'd finished with his other call and had come on over to offer assistance. He said the dispatcher had called him to say the trooper told her I might need a little help.

"How's the deer?" John asked, leaning out of his truck window.

"Good," I said, picking a pine needle out of my collar. "Mark cured her. Runs good. I think she'll be fine."

John, being a good friend, nodded and looked down at his steering wheel, trying to hide a big grin. From the look on his face, I guessed my deer tracking effort had been hot news on the police scanner that night.

"Okay then, Eric. Glad to see you're safely out of the woods. You and Mark have a good night. Guess I'll head home too."

I thanked John again, turned the key in the ignition and headed home. Mark was asleep beside me, still at last.

I ran into that same trooper a few of times over the years. He always made it a point to give me a big smile and wave and walk on over and ask about Mark.

I remember one time in particular. It was a week or so before Christmas and I was shopping for a few things over in Hardwick. It was dark and the streets were choked with snow.

I heard a "Hey, Warden!" shout from across the street followed by, "How's that dog?" and this big fellow came scooting over to talk to me.

I didn't recognize him at first, because, like me, he was out of uniform. But he sure knew me.

Before I could get a word out, he said, "I just had to come on over and say hello. You know, Warden, I've been to a few dog trials in my time. But I have never, ever seen a dog tracking exhibition before or since that could hold a candle to that night with you and Mark tracking that doe. Yes, indeedy, you two sure put on one heck of a show."

Quite a compliment, don't you think?

"But no deer took off. Mark followed his nose
to the biggest pine there, dove in behind it and
came out the other side carrying a wicker
creel in his mouth and grinning ear to ear."

Furry Fish Finder

Rumor had it that a couple of guys were taking substantially more than their fair share of brook trout over in the Elmore and Wolcott areas.

This is a pretty big area to cover given the number of feeder streams and brooks. So I resorted to a combination of canoe and footwork to see if I might catch the brook crooks.

This day I had strapped my solo canoe on top of the cruiser and took my dog, Mark, with me too. He loved to come along. Every once in awhile he was actually useful. But even when he wasn't, he was good company.

For instance, I had learned a long time ago if I was going to take him in a canoe with me, I had better be prepared to swim to shore. Mark was easily excited. He wasn't good at sitting still.

So, today I told Mark to guard the cruiser while I checked licenses for a bit. I parked my vehicle in the shade and left the cruiser with the windows all the way down for him to enjoy the breeze. I knew he would stay with the car and wait for me.

I was canoeing a series of deep water holes near Zack Woods Pond following up on my lead, when I remembered a trout stream over the hill. It meandered a half mile or more through some fallow farm fields. Good fishing. I beached my canoe in the brush at the edge of the pond and headed for the stream.

When I crested the hill, I spotted a couple of guys fishing down below me, along a patch of alders that leaned out over the edge of the stream. As I was up above them a good 500 feet and they were intent on their fishing, they had no idea I was watching them.

I stepped along the ridgeline, into a pine grove for cover and kept watching.

They were fishing maybe 50 feet apart from one another. I stood there a good half hour. They were both catching fish, doing exceptionally well, in fact.

Each had wicker creels at their sides. I stood and watched them another 45 minutes or more. I saw that every fish they caught went into their creels.

When most of us fish, we aren't that lucky. You always catch fish that are either too small or aren't in season and you have to put some back. Not these guys. Everything they caught was a keeper.

They were tag teaming it, fishing out one hole after another on this brook, and it looked to me like they were just stripping it of fish. There would not be much left for anyone else to catch.

I kept my distance and moved along parallel to them on top of the hill as they continued their casting and catching. I was adding up the number of fish they deposited in their creels.

After about twenty minutes, I saw the fellow in a blue nylon jacket pocket eight fish. When he hooked his ninth fish, I saw him look left, then right over his shoulder. When he saw the coast was clear, he slid the fish into his front coat pocket.

Definitely up to no good, I thought.

A couple minutes later I saw the pair meet up and have a brief conversation. I couldn't hear the words, but I knew all three of us would be chatting shortly.

The taller male proceeded downstream while the

angler in the blue windbreaker turned around and headed towards the pines where I was standing.

I had good cover for watching from a distance but I knew it wouldn't hold up if this fellow kept coming straight at me. I was certain he would spot me. There was nothing but open space between us.

I froze like a mud turtle on a river log on a summer day, and hoped this guy would just think I was another tree.

He stopped a little off to the left of me, maybe 30 yards away, looked behind him, took off his creel and coat, laid down his pole and walked another 10 feet or so straight towards me. He stopped just in front of the pines where I was hiding.

He unbuckled his belt, dropped his trousers right in front of my eyes and proceeded to answer Nature's call as innocent as a four month old puppy. His eyes got that glazed dreamy look as he focused on the job. The only thing missing was the floppy ears.

This was uncomfortable.

The guy was looking right at me, just not seeing me.

What to do?

I don't recall my police academy instructors
covering this particular occurrence: how
to introduce yourself to a stranger who is
defecating on your doorstep as it were.

I tried not to look, like you do taking your dog
out for a walk in the city. But I had to keep my
eyes open. I was afraid if I blinked he would see
me. I was frozen and formulating my greeting
when I saw the fog slowly lift from the half-
naked man's face.

His mouth fell open. He lept straight up in the
air from his squat, fell forward a step, reached
down, grabbed his trousers with both hands and
hiked 'em up to his waist. Then with a quick
look over his shoulder and down the hill, he
smiled big and shouted, "Why, Hello Warden!"
and proceeded to buckle his belt.

He might be blind, but he wasn't stupid. He had
shouted out that greeting for a reason and we
both knew it.

The tall guy on the brook down below heard
him shout, looked up and saw me in uniform
standing just 10 feet above his fishing partner.

The angler on the stream didn't hesitate. He

pointed his pole in front of him, pressed his creel to his side with his other hand and took off like a gazelle with a leopard on his tail downstream and away from me.

I trotted the couple big steps down to the shouter, ordered him to show me his license, open his creel and empty all his pockets.

There were 12 trout in his creel and a lot of fish slime inside the coat pockets. He was right at the daily limit. I took his fishing license and told him to stay put, I would be back.

Then I ran down the hill after his buddy who had made it clear around the bend out of sight. I knew there was a road that intersected this stream maybe a quarter mile from here. I thought maybe they had a car parked there and this guy would just drive off.

I got to the bend as quick as I could and expected to have to keep running to the road, but instead, there was my suspect, walking towards me with his fishing pole in his hand like he didn't have a care in the world. Like he hadn't just bolted away from me.

"Well, Hello, Warden. How you doing today? Nice day, hunh?" he said and smiled slyly.

"Yes, lovely," I said, like a knife on a flint. This guy obviously wanted to play games.

"I'd like to see your license and see your fish, please."

The fellow produced a worn but valid fishing license. Then he pulled seven brook trout out of the back pockets of his jeans.

"Where is your creel?" I asked.

"Ain't got no creel," he answered.

"That's funny. You had one all the time I was watching you fish from up above on the hillside," I said.

"Ain't got no creel," he said again. He flapped his long arms up and down for emphasis like a heron and shrugged.

I took a step away from him and looked around. He must have hidden the creel along the brook edge or in the brush or trees near where we were standing. There was a lot of ground to search.

If I could find the hidden creel while the fish where still fresh, I'd have my case. No way this guy wasn't over the legal daily limit.

"Okay, have it your way," I said. "I'll just take your information here and when I find your creel I'll pay you a little visit, and bring you a citation."

I got my pen and pad out and took down all the information from him about where he lived, where he worked, driver's license and fishing license info. Then I told him to stay put, walked back around the bend and waved the other fellow down from off the hill. When he arrived, I took the same information from him.

Every once in awhile I looked up and when I did, I made mental notes about where the three of us were standing. And I made a point of digging my heels into the earth a bit to mark the spot too. I wanted to be able to find it easily when I came back.

"Where you fellows parked?" They told me they were down at the road.

"Well, why don't I just walk you on down to your vehicle," I suggested. They didn't refuse.

I wanted them both out of there so I could start my search for the missing creel.

I escorted them to their vehicle and as they settled in, I had some time to look through the glass inside their car.

I figured the tall fellow would not have had time to run back to the car, stash his creel inside and run back to greet me and not break a sweat. Still, I looked through the front and back windows of their car anyway without being too obvious. No sign of the creel.

I also guessed the smart aleck would return to retrieve his creel at some point. But I figured he wouldn't be so dumb as to circle back immediately. He knew I'd be searching for it. If they were coming back, they would wait until just before dark. I wanted to find that creel before they did.

So, as soon as they drove out of sight, I took off too.

I knew I hadn't a prayer of finding that creel all by myself. There were too many places to stow it in the tall grass, under the edge of the stream bank, between some rocks or up in the berry bushes at the tree line. Acres of choices.

I needed to get my secret weapon—Mark the wonder dog.

As some of you may have read earlier, Mark was a veritable hunting machine, as long as there weren't distractions like food, toys, guns going off, deer, other dogs, birds, rabbits or basically anything that might possibly interest him.

Mark was a star in the yard at home with me—he was great at finding and bringing back toys. But as a retriever in the real world, sometimes he choked.

He got too excited or confused or could not handle the stress or all of the above. If he had been a human athlete, I guess he might have been diagnosed with attention deficit disorder or performance anxiety—or both.

But the fact remained, every once in a blue moon, under the right conditions, Mark could be spectacular.

And today, I just had a feeling, could be Mark's day. Maybe Mark could be my fish finder. I needed some sort of miracle to find that creel. It was a needle in a haystack in all that open space.

I hotfooted it back over the hill, down to my canoe and paddled back to the cruiser. Mark woke up and was his usual jumping for joy self at my return. I let him out to pee while I strapped the canoe to the roof rack and gave him the good news we had a job to do.

Then I drove quickly to the connecting road

where I had seen the scofflaws drive away about 45 minutes earlier.

I parked my cruiser and kept Mark on a lead until we got to the spot where I chatted with the "Ain't got no creel" fellow. I urged Mark to give that spot a good sniff, to start working, asking him to "Hunt 'er up," hoping Mark would get a big snoot full of that poacher's boots, pants, jacket, fish slime and the missing creel.

I was praying a deer was not sleeping anywhere nearby in the tall grass. If there was a deer, Mark would almost certainly forget all about following fish scent. Mark's first love was deer, pure and simple.

If Mark failed me, I would have to resort to Plan B. Plan B was stumble around acres of ground and hope for a miracle. My money was on my dog.

I was thinking a creel must look a lot like a toy to a dog and maybe Mark would find it and bring it back to me. Just maybe. I had never taught Mark to go sniffing for fish, but he liked to eat fish. If I had some left over trout or salmon on my plate, he would get it, lick his chops and want more.

So maybe this would work. I really had no idea.

But I knew the alternative was for me to get on my hands and knees scouring a couple acres of ground and I didn't think that was going to work.

Of course, I was also taking a chance Mark might eat the evidence if he did find it. But desperate times call for desperate measures. And I really wanted to nail these guys.

The smug grin on the "Ain't got no creel" angler's face really bothered me.

I watched Mark put his nose to the ground and wag his tail and sniff. He began running in large, ever widening circles. He would run and then come in to me, panting and looking for a pat on the head. I would walk 20 feet or so and then send him out again with the words, "Hunt 'er up!"

That was the game we played at home and most often, he would find the scented toy. Today, it was the same game, only the stakes were real. I wanted to stop these guys from stealing fish.

Over and over I kept Mark moving in the hope he would stumble onto the creel and bring it back to me.

I kept thinking the fellow could not have gone far

to hide the fish basket. He was out of my sight
only a couple of minutes. I had looked at his
hands while chatting with him. There was no
sign of any dirt under his fingernails indicating
he had buried the creel.

We had been on the search for a half hour
or more when Mark suddenly froze on the
hillside just above me, put his nose closer to
the ground and took off in a straight line with
his tail wagging towards a small stand of white
pines maybe another 60 feet up the hillside.
I stood back and held my breath—afraid
maybe he saw a deer in there and I was about
to lose him.

But no deer took off. Mark followed his nose
to the biggest pine there, dove in behind it and
came out the other side carrying a wicker creel
in his mouth and grinning ear to ear.

I was as happy as he was—happier probably.

I called his name and encouraged him to bring
it right to me—I didn't want him to get any
ideas about opening up this "toy" and eating the
goodies inside.

He trotted right on down the hill to me and I
caught the creel just as he was about to drop it
at my feet.

I managed to keep the lid latched before taking it from him. I was still concerned he might eat the evidence.

With one hand rubbing Mark's ears and telling him what a good dog he was, I bent one knee and rested the creel on it, flipped open the lid and started counting.

There were 38 fish in that creel. Even if I gave the grinning heron credit for a full day's catch, he was still way over the limit. How many more fish would this guy have taken if I hadn't stopped them? How many had he been routinely stealing?

I flipped the lid down on the creel and put it over my shoulder. Mark wanted me to throw it, to keep the game going. It was hard to explain to Mark that I couldn't toss it to him and he could not have one or two of the fish inside. I tried to make it up in praise and pats. When we got back to the cruiser, I gave him an old tennis ball to chew on.

The next day, I swung by the shop where both men worked. I walked in holding the wicker fish basket out in front of me. The wise guy who had ditched the creel less than 24 hours earlier wasn't smiling now. He was speechless in fact. No way did he think I would find it.

"Recognize this?" I opened the lid, reached

inside and handed him a citation.

His buddy couldn't contain himself. "How'd you ever find it?" he asked in disbelief.

I just smiled. I wouldn't give them the satisfaction of telling him how I did it.

A few weeks later, I got word the smirker would not contest the charges. The fish in the area had caught a break. I hoped his buddy—who just escaped being over the day's limit—got the message too.

I called a friend with a private pond and came home with a mess of trout that night. I cooked up a big fish fry for the family. Mark got his own big plate with several trout cooked just for him.

As I watched Mark savor his meal and wag his tail I grinned in satisfaction. I thought of my fellow warden in southern Vermont who told big stories about his lab's deer tracking prowess.

Deer tracking dog? Heck, they're common. But a fish tracking dog? No one had one but me.

Yup, Mark was one of a kind.

"I'm yelling to you, 'Warden, turn around!
Get outta there! I can see from the rustling
tassels above you that you are headed right for
the bear. Geezum Crow! I thought you
were going to bump into him.'"

BEAR? *WHERE???*

I got a call from a farmer named Dave over in the Garfield Flats area of Hyde Park. He told me his corn crop was getting hammered and he thought bears were the problem.

I needed to pay a visit.

I drove over to talk to Dave. It wasn't a chore.
His was an idyllic Vermont farm, pretty as a
postcard.

There were hundreds of unbroken acres of
mixed beech and hardwoods interspersed with
hemlock and swamp bordering Dave's land. The
good cover here offered the shy, solitary bears
food in all seasons and the ability to access it
safely.

Trouble is, sometimes Mother Nature comes up
short. This particular year it looked like the
beechnut and acorn crops black bears count on
to fatten up for their winter hibernation was cut
about in half.

I saw that Dave's corn patch was planted about
10 feet from a treed, gently sloping hillside. That
made it a very tempting walk from the woods
into the sweet corn for raccoons, deer, bears or
any hungry animal. Dave's corn patch consisted
of acres of cow corn and a smaller piece of sweet
corn to sell and feed his family.

Dave told me the sweet corn would be ready
in the next few days if the sunny weather held
steady. He was eager to harvest the sweet corn,
as he had a number of area restaurants and

grocery stores waiting. But if whatever was thrashing through this patch kept up its nightly visits, he would lose a good share of his product and profit. He said he had some trouble the last two years, but this particular growing season it was out of control. He was ready to aim and fire.

I stood outside my truck at the farm house. Dave had a nice big red barn a few feet away, with the corn a quarter-mile away below us. All looked well from the front of the corn patch as we stood talking and watching the swaying tassels below. But Dave explained the damage was hidden in the back and we needed to walk down to see the downed stalks and beat-up, uneaten ears of corn wasting on the ground.

I told him I wanted my shotgun with me and walked to my truck, grabbed the gun, and put some slugs in my pocket. My pistol was on my hip as well. We walked down the farm road together to stand inches away from corn stalks straight and tall, with a fair number of fat ears on each stalk.

But as we made a wide arc to approach the wooded side of the corn patch, I clearly saw what Dave was talking about—there were living room-sized patches of flattened stalks, dozens of ears of corn busted up and chewed—a lot of damage for a farmer who survives on thin margins even in a good year. A lot more damage than raccoons or deer would do. From the looks of the mess, it was black bears.

When a bear walks into a corn patch it flattens everything in its path. They are a tank with paws. But they don't necessarily eat everything they see. They can be as picky with their food as an anorexic Hollywood starlet in search of the perfect lettuce leaf lunch. They will knock down a corn stalk with a half dozen ripe ears and take just a few bites from one ear and leave the rest, then move on and do it all over again.

Come fall, when a bear's instincts tells him to bulk up for the lean winter months of hibernation ahead, bears are positively mad about food—climbing beech and oak trees, rummaging through their favorite berry patches for remnants, and in lean nut years, raiding beehives and farmers' corn fields.

This was a lean nut year for the bears in this valley. Unable to get what it needed from the woods, a bear had sniffed the breeze, smelled ripening corn and dove in. Could even be a mama bear with cubs. Tough to see tracks in this mess of downed corn stalks.

There are biologists who believe bears can smell bird seed sitting in a single bird feeder in the spring from a mile or more away. If that is true, what must acres of ripening corn smell like to a bear with the nose of a bloodhound? It must be the equivalent of a midnight diner on a long lonely interstate flashing a "Meatloaf, mashers and gravy like Mama used to make" sign to a 350-pound trucker who hasn't eaten for two days. Irresistible.

For all the same reasons Dave wanted to feed and fatten his dairy cows with corn in the coming winter, one or more bears were stripping his corn stalks and beating the cows in the barn out of their lunch come February.

And while black bears are mostly nocturnal, I also knew all bets were off at this time of year. Their ravenous urges will drive them to do what they would not do at any other time of year, including gorge themselves in a corn field in the middle of a sunny day.

So that's why Dave and I proceeded cautiously. I had a feeling the bruin, maybe one with cubs, just might be in that acreage feeding, despite the bright sunshine.

I advised Dave to keep his eyes on the corn stalk tops. "Look for any unusual movement and

sounds," I said. Dave nodded. We whispered
and continued on our path, leaned our heads
way back and scanned the tassels for a good
10 minutes or so.

There was a gentle intermittent breeze, but
not so much that we wouldn't notice a large
presence rustling through the corn. And sure
enough, after about 15 minutes of walking, Dave
saw tassels swaying out near the middle of the
sweet corn section that we couldn't attribute to
the slight breeze. He jerked his head towards
me and pointed to the spot. I nodded and we
both stopped in our tracks and listened. Maybe
I was just imagining it, but I could swear I heard
some chewing.

The problem was that as we walked on up closer
to the corn rows, to sneak up on whatever the
creature was in there, the height of the stalks
and all those crinkly corn leaves reaching out
along the rows totally obstructed our view.

What to do?

At 6 foot tall for me and a little less for Dave,
neither of us had much of a chance of seeing
above the corn and tracking the stalks moving
around us. Just stumbling around in there
could get us into real trouble if my suspicions
about a bear in the corn patch were correct.

I whispered to Dave to stop. This wasn't safe.

I turned and he followed me until we were back
up about 500 feet away from the edge of the
corn patch at the foot of the little rise to the
barn. There, Dave and I concocted a game plan.

I was the guy with the gun and the uniform, so
I was going in. No question about that. The
question was, just how I was going to be able
to keep my bearings and see anything once I
walked back on down there and entered the corn
patch? The sweet corn stalks were a good seven
feet high or better and the cow corn stalks were
another foot or two higher still. All those corn
stalks kinda look alike once you are inside. How
was I going to spot whatever critter was in there
chowing down on Dave's corn?

As we watched the unusual motion in the corn,
I tried to estimate the distance to the spot and
how many rows I had to walk through to get
near whatever was doing the damage. I came
up with a guesstimate of about 150 feet from the
trees and 60 rows in.

I told Dave he should just stay put but if he
could direct me from the spot we were standing
with hand signals or shouts if necessary that
that would be nice. I didn't really expect that
to work, but I thought it would keep him busy

up on the hillside and stop him from walking on down there trying to help.

I was fine walking a straight line down to the sweet corn with my shotgun across my chest and my .357 in my holster. Still I had to admit it was a little spooky walking into the corn. I had to take a deep breath and remind myself that there hadn't been a case of a black bear hurting, let alone killing, someone in Vermont in 100 years or more. Just how threatened would a black bear be if I stumbled on it out here while it was gorging itself on sweet corn? I hoped I didn't have to find out.

I wanted to see the bear to determine the age and condition of the intruder. If it had an ear tag, I might be able to narrow it down as to whether it was a bruin the Department had dealt with before.

I was swallowed up by the corn stalks within three rows. There was corn everywhere. And it was a lot noisier than I thought it would be inside the patch. Rustling, drying leaves rubbed against other stalks. Trying to squeeze through rows of corn wasn't a noiseless operation. Every footfall resulted in a rustle in my ears as the sharp-edged, paper thin leaves swooshed and crinkled. At the same time, the corn tassles turned the sunlight above me into a kind of disco ball of spotlights and shadows. It was tough to figure out which direction I was headed.

I tried to keep my internal compass on track by counting the rows I crossed, and hoping the bruin I was searching for was holding still while I believed I was sneaking up on him. But as I tried to cut across rows to get to where I thought the bear was, confusion began to set in. Had I gone 100 feet forward and 30 east or where was I exactly? I felt my palms getting a little wet and a trickle of sweat slid down my neck.

I thought I heard a shout behind me but the rustling of the corn stalks made it impossible to decipher the message. Was it Dave up on the hill shouting to me? There was no way I could see him, or shout back. I was a prisoner of the corn and I didn't want to blow my cover.

I decided I needed to stand still and take a look around to get my bearings. But you can't climb a corn stalk. I figured my best bet was to jump. Jump up and down in all four directions and see what I could see in that split second. I just might be able to rise above the corn and get my bearings.

I had seen plenty of television specials where dancers leap from a standing position two feet or

more straight up. And, of course, who doesn't
love to see a basketball player do a jump shot
from the foul line? They make it look so easy.
Well, let me tell you, it isn't. Especially when
you have a shotgun in your left hand, a .357 on
your hip and a 45-year-old body.

I jumped and looked and all I saw was corn
and a bit more sunlight. No sign of Dave. So, I
turned a quarter of a circle and jumped again.
Same thing. Then again. Each time all I saw
was sunlight and corn. I did this until I figured
I had north, east, south and west pretty well
covered.

There was no sign of Dave and there was no
pause button I could hit to freeze my jump at
the top of the arc and look around like some
cartoon character. My body was no match
for gravity. All I got out of the jumping was a
cramp in my right calf and corn silk covering my
shoulders, dangling from the bill of my cap and
sliding into my shirt collar.

As I stood there trying to decide what to do next,
I heard something—a kind of low blowing sound
maybe 100 feet away. Once, twice.

The hair on the back of my neck rose up like
an old bear hound. I froze, but my hand went
instinctively to my shotgun safety. I lowered

the muzzle of my gun and stood still. I looked
in the direction of the sound.

I couldn't see anything but corn. Was I
imagining the sound of a bear huffing?

From above me off in the distance somewhere
I now heard another shout—muffled yelps, not
from a dog, but a human voice. Was that Dave
trying to tell me something? I couldn't make out
a word.

Geezum Crow. What is going on?

My mind raced trying to come up with a solution
here. Should I walk towards where I thought
the huffing noise was? Should I walk away from
it? Should I just chuck this whole idea given the
fact I can't see anything but corn stalks and just
run like hell? Which way?

As I stood there trying to decide, I heard the
noise again. A blowing sound off in the corn.
No chewing. No rustling. I know bears sound
alarms when they feel threatened and will try
and bluff. Was this a bear bluffing or was it
getting ready to charge me?

I bent my knees and slowly slid straight down.
I thought if I got low in the stalks I could look
down the rows just above the earth and there

would be less greenery and maybe I could see better. No dice. It didn't work. The bear could be 50 feet or 100 feet away. Or maybe I was just hearing something else. The sound of the rustling wind in the corn still drowned out most everything.

It was clear to me if it was a bear, the bruin had a distinct advantage. They have a great nose. Mine was only human.

I decided to give jumping a try again. One final leap to see if it would help me at least choose a direction to try and walk out. I put the safety back on the shotgun and jumped, looking for any clearing in the corn, a boundary of grass to corn that I might head towards or something to get my bearings.

And that's when I saw the flash of a big black head and shoulders towering over the corn, looking right at me.

"BEAR!!!," my mind screamed.

When I hit the earth this time I ducked down and pointed the shotgun barrel straight out before me and slipped the safety off. How far away was the bear? I tried to estimate it from my split second view of the bruin. Was it coming at me?

Again, I could hear the distant sound of a human voice away and to the left. Gotta be Dave up there. I would be better off with smoke signals at this stage.

Now, I have no clue where I am inside the rows of corn. I have twisted and turned a couple of times. And if the bear decides to rush me, I could be all done before the shotgun muzzle ever clears these corn stalks and I get a shot off.

Time to go. But first, I had to jump up and try and see if I could determine which way was the door out of this corn patch.

I jumped up again and looked. And again, I saw a big black head and shoulders standing above the corn patch, apparently looking for me.

With my senses on high alert and my neck swiveling from side to side like it was on greased casters, I began backing up as quietly as I could, my finger on the trigger.

At thirty paces I froze and listened again. I decided I had to jump again in case I was being followed and to make certain I wasn't going deeper into the corn patch.

Again on the hillside I heard yelling but

could not make out the words. My heart was pounding. I tried sniffing the breeze as if I was a bear. All I smelled was corn and wet earth. I listened for unusual rustling, looked for any flash of black or brown—nothing. Just corn, countless stalks of corn all around me.

I decided I gotta get outta here now. I backed up another 20 paces, faster this time, swallowed hard, took a deep breath and jumped up again. Is that something black off in the distance above the corn stalks or am I just imagining things? Am I getting away from the bear? I thought the trees are getting bigger, which meant I was closer to the hillside and headed for an exit.

I decided to crab walk sideways through the stalks, my shotgun still at the ready, but the muzzle down.

I thought I was headed towards Dave and away from the bear. After 30 crab steps I stopped and took a deep breath and lept up, trying to see where I was. To my relief, I saw a flash of red tractor and the barn looked bigger. I was almost home free.

When I slipped out of the corn patch, I grinned and breathed a big sigh of relief. I saw Dave a couple hundred feet away waving both arms

over his head like he worked on an aircraft
carrier. He was grinning broadly. I looked
behind and around me to make certain I hadn't
been followed. I put on a confident smile, put
the safety back on the shotgun and headed up
towards Dave.

"Eric. Didn't you see the bear?" Dave called
down to me as I approached him. Dave then
proceeded to tell me about the Laurel and Hardy
show the bear and I had put on for the past half
hour.

"First the bear popped up and it's a BIG one,"
he said laughing and shaking his head like he
couldn't believe what he saw. Dave's eyes open
wide and his arms spun like windmill vanes.

"I'm yelling to you, 'Warden, turn around!
Get outta there! I can see from the rustling
tassels above you that you are headed right for
the bear. Geezum Crow! I thought you were
going to bump into him.'"

"Then I see you popping out of the corn patch
like a Jack in the Box. It's like I'm watchin' a
puppet show. You jump up and look around.
Then the bear stands up and looks around.
Each of you taking turns. Wish I'd a had my
camera. Did you get a look at him? That's a
big bear!"

Relieved I had survived the corn maze, Dave couldn't get the whole story out fast enough, just busting to share what he'd seen. Apparently, I had been closer to real danger than I knew.

"I got a glimpse," I said nonchalantly. "Mostly what I saw was corn."

"Well, it's a BIG bear," Dave says again. "That cow corn generally runs 8 feet tall or more, and that bear was a good foot or two taller than that when he was standing up looking around for you."

Sure glad I didn't pop up next to him, I was thinking. But I tried to act as though I do this daily. I took a deep breath.

"Well, Dave, we definitely know you have a problem here and if you don't mind I'll put in a call to a friend who hunts bear with dogs and ask him to come on down here and put his dogs on the scent for you. It should scare the bear enough to chase him up into the woods where he belongs, and keep him from coming down here and eating your corn. How's that sound?"

Dave said that would be fine as long as it worked. Deer in the freezer were good eating, he said, but he was not a fan of bear meat. As long as the bear left his crops alone he would leave it alone.

We headed back up towards the barn and my truck and Dave just kept chuckling to himself and shaking his head.

"Eric, I hate to lose corn, but I gotta tell you what I saw today was something I will never forget. That bear standing above the corn and you jumping up and down looking for him—the both of you maybe 50 feet apart. Wow! Can't wait to tell the boys at breakfast."

Uh oh. I knew what that meant. Most all the farmers and area craftsmen gathered for coffee between 4 and 5:30 am at the Charlemont before heading off to work. I could see I was going to be a hot topic of conversation tomorrow. Dave knew a lot of people. Oh well, part of the joy of being a public servant is you have to be able to take the kidding with the kudos.

Sure enough, two days later I pulled in for coffee and a sandwich around noon. The diner was a good place for a quick lunch and to catch up on the news as well. I'd even gotten some good tips there in the past.

Patty, a young waitress with a spring in her step, was waiting tables today. I ordered my usual burger and coke and started chatting with a fellow I knew about fishing on the Lamoille River.

About 10 minutes later, a big meaty hand slid a heavy china plate beneath my nose with my burger sitting pretty before me.

Next to the burger was a steaming ear of sweet corn slathered in butter and salt in place of the usual potato chips. I looked up from my lunch to let my server know I didn't order any corn, when I saw a guy in a cook's apron, about 325 pounds. It was Brian, the cook.

He saw the puzzled look on my face and said, "A gift from your friend in Dave's corn patch," drew his hairy tattooed cook's arms up sharp and fast over his head, spread his sausage fingers wide like bear paws, roared, clawed at the air a few strokes, turned and walked off.

The entire lunch crowd cracked up.

I felt my face turn red. I reached for the hot ear of corn. I gingerly picked it up in both hands, my pinkies pointing out like I was taking tea with the queen.

I smiled at my audience very briefly, ducked my chin and took a couple big bites.

There was applause and some hooting. I didn't dare look up—in case someone had a camera. I reached for a napkin with my left hand and with my right I waved the cob at my audience and smiled sheepishly. Inside I was dying, of course. But I was hoping the diners would forget about me quickly if I just played along.

I was right. In a few more painful seconds the diners returned to their conversations and ignored me. I was left to enjoy my lunch.

I took a few bites from my burger, and then returned to the sweet corn. The ear had cooled a bit. This time I could really savor it.

And it was then it struck me. Dave's sweet corn was some of the tastiest I'd eaten in years.

Smart bear.

"Jane was standing hunched over on
the stair landing below. Her hair was a
mess; her nightgown was splattered with
dark red stains. In her shaking hands,
she held some mud colored lumps."

SQUISH IN THE NIGHT

Being married to a game warden is not for the faint of heart.

This is one of the stories that became legend in our family and just might have had something to do with why my first wife, Jane, and I are no longer married.

It was the 1970s. There was an economic Recession going on and my underemployed brother, Gene, was living up the road from us in Eden.

One of the sideline jobs the department allowed wardens to do was salvage deer hides. The skins are used to make all manner of products—gloves and moccasins, to name two. A warden could sell or barter the skins from dead deer. It wouldn't bring in a lot of money, but it was something extra.

Gene wanted more income. He and I made a deal. I would pick up road-killed deer and drop them off at his place. Gene—like a lot of back-to-the earth types in the 70s—was going through a Native American phase at the time. Being able to gut and skin deer was considered a good survival skill to have in your repertoire.

Gene said he'd read the heart and liver were the most nutritious part of the animal and prized by Native Americans. He liked to include these organs as part of his regular diet.

With my supervisor's approval, Gene and I agreed he would clean the deer I picked up, take the heart and liver and whatever innards he wanted to eat, keep the hide, and I would take the carcass and sell it for meat. Needy local families got venison, the Department got some money, Gene got to eat and trade the hides for a little extra income. Everybody won.

But sometimes the best plans go awry.

So it was that one particularly long day, I pulled into Gene's yard, dead tired at 2 am with yet another road-killed deer in the back of my pickup. It was my third such retrieval in as many days.

Gene was up processing a deer from the

night before. He liked working at night. As
we unloaded the carcass, Gene insisted on
wrapping up a liver for me to take home for
dinner the next night.

"Good for you, Brother. Best part of the deer,"
he said. "Heck, this liver will put iron in your
blood." I was too tired to argue.

A few minutes later I pulled into my driveway. I
grabbed my gear bag and the liver, locked up the
truck and stumbled into the house.

I plopped the liver down in the kitchen sink,
then walked back to the mudroom, hung
up my coat and secured my weapon. I was
planning to put the liver in the refrigerator, but
I forgot all about it in the few steps back to the
mudroom.

A couple of the ever-present house cats snaked
around my ankles as I headed for the stairs. I
didn't think anything of it. I had learned to
shuffle around them. I knew the kids or Jane
would feed them in the morning. I bent down
and gave one a quick pat and padded in my
socks up to bed.

I'd been asleep maybe three hours when I heard
it: a blood curdling scream followed by a ka-
bumpa, bumpa, thumpa-thumpa and then a

final THUD and a moan.

What the....?

I sat up board-straight in bed, my eyes
wide open, my brain not yet engaged, and
instinctively reached for the night stand, threw
open the drawer, and grabbed my pistol.

I looked beside me for Jane. She was gone. I
listened harder.

And then I heard it, a woman's moan followed
by a stream of crescendo-like cursing that was
so fast and furious it was more like speaking in
tongues.

I lowered the pistol and reached for the light and
climbed out of bed. The cursing and muttering
ended in a beller of "ERIC!" and I knew now that
whatever had occurred outside the bedroom
door, somewhere outside my perfect world of
badly needed sleep, I had screwed up.

The fog of sleep was beginning to lift.

I could tell from Jane's tone that I didn't need
the revolver. I put the gun back inside the
drawer, dashed to the top of the stairs, flipped
the light switch on, and looked down.

Jane was standing hunched over on the stair
landing below. Her hair was a mess; her
nightgown was splattered with dark red stains.
In her shaking hands, she held some mud
colored lumps.

She looked like Lady Macbeth. It was clear Jane
didn't know whether to scream or cry or both.

"Eric!" she hissed and shook a foot in rage.

It was tough to see in the dim light, but
suddenly I got it.

"Oh my gosh, the liver!" I thought to myself.
"But what? Who?"

"Jane, are you all right?" I asked and began
trotting down the stairs to meet her.

But when I hit the third step, I stepped on
something squishy and slippery. My foot went
out from under me and I fell backwards. I
caught myself and skidded like a skateboarder
on my heels over another couple treads and
almost landed on top of Jane. The handrail
saved me.

I took a deep breath and turned to look behind
me to see if someone had buttered the stairs.

That was when I saw the carnage. There were
bits of chewed meat scattered about the stair
treads like a minefield. I turned back towards
Jane, squinted and peered off towards the
kitchen. It wasn't pretty. There was torn up
butcher paper strewn from the kitchen sink all
the way through the living room and on up to
Jane and me.

What the ?

And then it struck me: CATS!

Even worse, cooperating cats. Because to
get that big hunk of liver out of the sink and
chew and drag it all over the house took more
than one cute little kitty cat. We were talking
organized jungle cats, a pride of skilled hunters.

Maybe the house lions had wanted to share
their kill with us? Maybe they wanted to store
their booty in a tree and figured the second story
was a good substitute? Maybe they planned to
butter the stairs with deer liver to trip me up?
Maybe they wanted to get my liver too?

I will never know.

I turned back to focus on Jane. She was
hopping from one foot to the other. I was

concerned she had really hurt herself. Then I realized it was probably just the creepy feel of bloody, raw deer liver stuck between her toes, sticking her feet to the stair treads that was the most profound source of her unhappy dance. I was wanting to jig and shake the butcher paper and bloody cat-chewed liver bits from my feet myself. But I had to stay calm.

As Jane's eyes got bigger, I had to confess. "It's deer liver is all. The cats must have gotten into it. I'm sorry. I'll get the mop and I'll clean it up." I said. "Are you okay?"

Jane nodded that she was all right, but I could see a few tears in her eyes. I didn't know if it was just from the fright and the mess or maybe she sprained her back or stubbed a toe.

I reached for the pieces of liver in her hand and removed the gluey globs gently. I looked Jane in the eye, gave her my best mea culpa, I am really sorry look, followed by a slight smile that begged forgiveness.

I waited.

Jane sighed and she didn't hit me. I took that as forgiveness, at least for the moment.

The four kids appeared, standing bleary-eyed and confused at the top of the stairs. They had never heard such a commotion in our house. Well, not in the middle of the night, anyway. The oldest took a step to head down the stairs, prompting me to turn and shout, "Stay back! Deer guts on the stairs!"

Our kids were used to seeing all kinds of animals about the place. Sometimes the animals were alive, sometimes not. So, our kids didn't get upset. They just stared at Jane and me, then at each other and waited for directions.

"I just have to clean up is all. Everything's fine. Just go on back to bed," I said.

I gave Jane a peck on the cheek and slid past her. I was headed to the kitchen for cleaning supplies. I wanted to get things tidied up before Jane had time to think more about all this kitty carnage. I mean, it wasn't like the cats went to the deli and bought their own deer liver. This was my fault.

The kids waited to hear from their mom. Jane spoke for the first time since her blood-curdling screams. Her voice was calm and steady—for the sake of the children, I was sure.

"I'm fine. We're fine. Just go on back to bed. It's not time to get ready for school yet," she said. I was relieved to hear her talk. I figured she would make a full recovery. The foursome turned and tottered back to bed.

I came back from the kitchen with rags, towels, a bucket of soapy water and a scrub brush. I bent down and wiped Jane's feet in silence. Then I scooted ahead and quickly wiped a path for Jane to walk up the stairs and back to bed without fear of deer liver sticking to her feet.

Jane's shoulders softened and she sighed. She limped up the stairs—carefully sidestepping some spots I had missed.

I followed the blood trail just like I would do in the woods. I turned on the lights, bent low and worked my way from the kitchen sink across the kitchen floor to the living room and up the stairs with soapy water, the brush and a mop. I got it all cleaned up as fast and as well as a sleep-deprived man could.

The sun was just peeking over the hill when I headed back up to bed.

Standing at the top of the stairs, I peered down into the living room and took a good long look

at my prime suspects: four exceptionally fat
bellied, deeply sleeping felines. As ever, they
were silently shedding all over the best furniture
in our home. The overstuffed chairs, our sofa,
the loveseat, even the dog's bed sported a smug
slumbering cat.

I looked hard at the pusses on those pusses.
I was trained to read signs of guilt in human's
faces, not cats. But it seemed to me each
of these animals had a look of immense
satisfaction on their faces and their stomachs
were distended more than usual at this early
hour. They looked to be smiling. There wasn't
the slightest trace of guilt or remorse on any
one of those feline faces.

I sighed and walked to our bedroom, slid into
bed beside Jane and slept soundly for a few
delicious hours.

Too soon, it was time to get up and get back to
work. I had promised to meet with some folks
over in Morrisville.

Before I left town, I swung by Gene's. I told him our cats agreed with him—deer liver was delicious, best part of the deer. And puh-lease, never, ever send me home with venison when I was half asleep.

I didn't think my marriage or my heart could take it.

*"Loosed from one snowshoe,
I was able to bob a bit higher in
the water and I felt encouraged.
My fingers were already
stiffening from the cold water.
Soon my hands would be numb
and useless."*

THIN ICE

I made it a priority to get out into the woods for at least an hour every day, no matter the weather, time of day or season.

If I could check a few hunting or fishing licenses or scout new territory while outside, great. If I didn't run into a hunter or angler on my walks, then I treated this time in the field like a training run to keep me in shape and my wilderness skills honed.

Being in the woods alone and in uniform wasn't without danger. First and foremost I had to keep in mind that I might come across some bruiser with a bad attitude who just might not want to be greeted by a man with a badge and some questions.

The longer you are in the job, the more citations you give out, the more poachers you nab and help prosecute over the course of your career, the greater the likelihood that you have made

some folks angry enough to fantasize about
retaliation.

I know wardens who have been retired for more
than a decade who never leave home without a
firearm—a rifle, shotgun, pistol or all three—in
their vehicle. They played fair but tough while
in uniform and they know they have made
enemies.

But realistically, it is the ever-changing weather
and the uncertain footing found in the Vermont
woods that can turn an hour or two excursion
into a life or death situation.

Take beaver marshes, for instance. The
level wet areas surrounding the dams look
benign—flat, often sedge and cattails growing
up, no open water, no obvious currents. Looks
like you could walk right across. But in
fact beaver marshes are notorious for being
treacherous, especially in winter.

Smooth ice covers the currents and beaver
passages. Snow falls on top of that ice. Slow
moving currents beneath the ice cut channels,
thinning the ice from the bottom up. Take a
walk and ice that looks safe from above collapses
beneath your step. In an instant you can be in
over your head and fighting for your life.

Crossing beaver ponds, streams and marshes in winter is an area where my partner, Torro, made a huge difference. For eight years of my career, this black Lab accompanied me on patrol in all seasons. Toro means bull in Spanish. I added the extra "r" for this pup because of his playful occasional grr-owl.

Torro was a good ambassador for the Department. A wagging tail and big lolling red tongue took away most of the fear the kids might have of me with my badge and gun.

But even better, Torro seemed to have a sixth sense about when not to appear like the neighbor's always friendly lab. If I approached someone in the woods or along a fishing hole to ask for proof of a license, he seemed to know it was time to get down to business. The tail wagging stopped. The big toothy grin changed to licking his chops. He would sit and stare at the person, waiting for my command. Any scofflaw remotely considering giving me some attitude, making a run for it, or taking a swing at me changed their mind when they glanced down at Torro. He was almost 100 pounds of solid muscle. He wasn't formally trained to be a police dog, but he sure had the instincts for it.

Torro lived for our daily woods patrols. His

favorite place was out in front of me exploring. And this brings me back to the subject of crossing water, ice and beaver marshes, which is where Torro was ultimately a lifesaver.

Torro was like any hunting dog, running out ahead of me, his head alternating between sniffing the air above his shoulders to lowering his nose a few inches above the ground. In winter, snowshoeing in and around marshes and ponds, if I saw him stumble and splash into water, I knew thin ice was ahead and stayed clear. Torro helped keep me safe.

There were several times in exploring new areas where Torro broke through ice atop a freshet or deep marsh I had not known was risky. He would generally bounce right back up, shake himself off and keep going. But if my foot had gone through in the same spot, it could have resulted in a nasty ankle sprain, ice bath or worse. Definitely not something you want happening on a cold day in January in the Vermont woods.

Being a lab, Torro was bred for water work. No matter what the temperature was, he loved water. He would shake it off, look back at me for reassurance, and keep forging ahead.

But there was one time Torro did take a bath

and I thought I might lose him. It was late
November. We were on a wounded deer track
following it around the edge of a small pond.
Torro got excited smelling that deer scent and he
took off, cutting across a corner of the pond in
front of us, rather than sticking closer to shore.
He got about 20 feet off shore and fell clear
through the ice. Gone.

I wasn't sure how deep the water was and waited
to see if he could get himself out, even as my
mind was racing to come up with a plan to
rescue him if I had to.

As I stood there holding my breath, I saw his
blocky black head bob out of the water above the
ice, then his front paws clawed the air and then
caught the edge of the ice out in front of him.

Torro scratched at the ice sheet while looking
at me, his shoulders pumping, his mouth wide
open and water flying out of the hole like a
geyser from his kicking back legs and flailing
front paws. As he clawed at the ice, the hole got
bigger. He was tearing up the thin ice in front
of him, headed towards shore, towards me, but
unable to set his rear feet down on something
solid that would allow him to leap out.

How long could he last? He was working hard. I
could see his haunches rise up as he propelled

himself forward. I heard desperate panting and the occasional yip as Torro struggled.

I called his name to encourage him and bent down and slapped my thighs and gripped my knees, willing him on.

I looked around for a downed tree or something I might crawl on to go out after him, even though I knew that would be foolish. Torro kept his eyes on me while paddling with his neck bent way back to keep his nose out of the water. He continued to claw with his front paws and pedal with his back legs. I saw he was using his chest to ram through the ice like a tug boat and making progress.

About 15 feet from shore, Torro managed to get his front paws on top of the ice. His neck was stretched out like a turkey. He dug his chin into the snow using his heavy head as an anchor.

I stood there trying to will him on. I saw his rib cage swell and he raised his head an inch or two off the ice, the water in the hole churned and he dug with his front claws in desperation.

It worked. He had found ice strong enough to support his body. Torro propelled himself forward and once his hind legs were free from the black water, he lay there like a walrus. He

was panting, exhausted, his legs splayed out. I
wanted to run onto the ice sheet and grab him.
But I knew the ice might give way under my
weight.

I waited.

Torro closed his eyes. His mouth was wide
open, gasping for air. His sides were heaving. I
stood up and looked at the spent dog on top of
the ice. Was that snow and ice on his muzzle
or white hairs? Maybe he just could not make
it the final few feet to me. Maybe Torro's heart
was giving out.

I was silently calling to him. "Torro, come on
old boy. Don't quit on me now. You can do it.
You're almost home. Come on, boy."

It was a long couple of minutes, but Torro began
to stir. His eyes opened. His head rose a few
inches from the ice on a wobbly neck. He began
to pull at the ice with his front paws, crawling
on his belly to me. His back legs were shaking
so badly he couldn't get onto his feet.

I knew he didn't have much left.

When he was about six feet from me, I took two
steps onto the ice, leaned over, slid my hand
under his collar, turned and ran to the shore

skidding him over the ice alongside me. The ice cracked beneath us, but it held.

I dropped to my knees and began to rub Torro down, to get his blood moving. He was a big, solid dog and I did not want him to go into shock and have to carry him out. I looked him over as I massaged him. He had torn a dew claw badly. His chest was rubbed raw in a few spots and seeping red from ramming the ice. His front pads were raw and bleeding. He began to shiver uncontrollably. I took off my jacket and then my thick winter shirt. I put my jacket back on and used my wool shirt like a towel for Torro. I massaged his trunk and rubbed his legs to get his circulation going for a good five minutes. Then I wrapped the shirt around him like a horse blanket. I knotted my shirt sleeves around his belly to keep it on him and got him to his feet and rubbed some more.

I knew Torro was out of the woods when he wagged his tail and licked my hands. When he stepped away from me and did the doggy shake, I took my shirt off him. That Labrador coat Mother Nature provided him was better than any blanket.

We left the deer track and headed back home. He was clearly exhausted walking out. Once home, I stoked the wood stove, pulled Torro's favorite dog bed closer to the stove and doctored his minor wounds. Torro was a little stiff the next few days, but he bounced right back.

That fall through the ice was the closest call Torro ever had out on the trail with me. I didn't realize until four years later how much I had learned watching him that day.

Torro had died the previous May, during turkey season. We'd had a couple good years after his fall through the ice. I hadn't found a dog to replace him.

I was on my own this clear blue sky January day, snowshoeing into a beaver dam. I was carrying forty pounds of Vermont's finest fisheries' water loaded with brook trout fry in a nice wicker backpack. The fry were inside a heavy plastic bag with a loose tie at the top, ready to be poured out all at once or in select locations I chose on my excursion.

The air temperature was below zero, but if I could pour the tiny fish and their watery bath into their new home at the same time, they wouldn't so much as chill a fin. They would eat and grow, and come early summer, they would be a good catch for back-country anglers. For angling purists, there is no better catch than brook trout. A sweet mountain brook ran right out of this marsh and those little fish would find it come spring and do fine.

We had a lot of snow that winter and to make the hike easier, I had chosen to wear my wooden snowshoes made by Tubbs—a Vermont classic. Ash frames, rawhide webbing and leather bindings. These snowshoes are narrower than the flattened, stretched-egg snowshoes most people use.

Each shoe was about 30 inches long, maybe 14 inches wide and sported a five-inch wooden tail. The design makes it easier to walk over powder, brush and marshes. The downside is the length can make it difficult to navigate tight turns in dense woods. My plan was to follow the shallow brook leading up to the beaver marsh where I planned to release the fry. The Tubbs were made for that.

The hike in was beautiful, with sunlight shining through bare branches and dappling the snow all around me with slices of gold and silver. The woods were mostly quiet with only the occasional call of a chickadee or a woodpecker hammering on a rotted tree. There were lots of fresh animal tracks. I enjoyed the walk and made good time.

In fact, I was having such a good time that I made a mistake.

It suddenly dawned on me that that the sun was really bright, blinding in fact. But if I was still on top of the brook ice, I would be in and out of sunlight and shadows.

Oops.

I hadn't been paying attention and my old friend Torro was not with me, running ahead and testing the ice for me.

I stopped, adjusted my pack straps and looked around. I had trekked right up onto the mouth of the beaver marsh, just where I did not want to be. The closest trees were a good 30 feet away to the east. I looked west and saw the shoreline was more like 100 feet away. East was my best bet. I needed to get off this marsh.

I took one cautious step towards the east shore. Then another. Just when I was thinking I had dodged a bullet, I heard a tremendous crack and plunged straight down into muddy water. It was so cold it took my breath away.

I was eyeball deep in muddy water, with shards of ice and powdery snow filling my eyes and slopping into my ears. My senses were in overload. I felt like I was being stabbed by a million icy nettles.

I rose up as high as I could from the muddy pond bottom. But my feet felt glued there. The leather snowshoe bindings allowed my heels to rise up three inches or so, but my toes were strapped in tight.

I knew I had to free my legs or I would never get out alive. I tried to kick my feet but the combination of mud, weeds and water was like trying to break free of wet cement.

The backpack wasn't helping.

I twisted and wriggled like an outraged bass on a hook. I worked it down my arms until it fell off my shoulders to the bottom. I caught glimpses of pieces of silver scooting out from the pack as it sunk. I guessed the fry had broken loose of the plastic bag.

How ironic would it be if the fish lived to see Spring and I didn't?

Freed from the pack, I thought I would gain a few inches, stand taller above the water line. I stretched my neck and reached for another breath. I quickly realized my wriggling had buried my snowshoes deeper in the muck, like an anchor.

I tried again to kick my feet—one at a time—to get the snowshoe bindings to release from my boots. I could not kick vigorously enough. The water, the marsh weeds, the mud and the current were all just too strong. I was going to have to dive down into the ice hole to release the leather bindings' buckles.

I took two deep breaths and with my eyes open and lips pursed hard, I squatted down into the water, brushed swaying slimy pond weeds away from my face, and reached for the bindings.

I managed to pry the binding off the back of my right boot before needing a breath. Loosed from one snowshoe, I was able to bob a bit higher in the water and I felt encouraged. My fingers were already stiffening from the cold water. Soon my hands would be numb and useless. I had to dive back under the water and free up the other shoe fast.

I bobbed once, twice and sucked in as much air as I could. I squat-dove back down into the ice and green gray ooze. I couldn't see a thing. But I felt my way around my boot heel. I tugged and pulled and twisted until I had my left boot free as well.

Free of my pack and the snowshoes, I blew out of that ice hole like a Beluga. But if I thought I could just land on solid ice and wriggle to shore, I was wrong. The ice was too thin to hold me up. It kept crumbling all around me and throwing me back into the water.

I would never make it to shore this way. And if I hit water much deeper, I would almost certainly drown.

That's when Torro pulling himself out of the marsh a few years earlier came into my head. "But I don't have paws and claws," I argued. "No, but you have snowshoes! Use 'em!"

Oh no! My snowshoes were on the bottom of the pond, a step or two behind me in the bottom of the marsh.

I needed those snowshoes.

I took three deep breaths and forced myself to squat down into the water once again, step back and reach behind me. I found one shoe and then the other. I jammed my fingers into the rawhide webbings and stood up tall.

I threw my right shoulder up and out and the snowshoe followed. The webbing went into the snow atop the ice and sunk an inch or two. It held me up. The ice did not break. I threw my left shoulder forward and out of the water. That shoe held too. Now I had two snowshoes sitting on the ice each with a numb hand stuck to them. At least my head was above water.

I paused. A slight smile crossed my cracked lips. This might actually work.

I threw my body forward, picked up one snowshoe at a time and slammed it as far ahead of me as I could without letting go. I kicked with both feet, alternated snowshoes and kept my eye on the shoreline.

I lost all sensation in my hands and feet. My fingers were little more than hooks. If a hand slid out of a snowshoe I would never be able to pick it up again.

Shards of broken ice slammed into my throat and sliced at my wrists. I dug my cheek into the ice, hoping maybe my 4 o'clock shadow would help me.

I was smashing a path through the ice with my chest, headed towards the tree line. My water-logged trousers and boots prevented me from jumping out onto the ice. The best I could do was wave my legs like a scuba diver wearing fins. I wanted to drop my feet to the pond bottom, but I was afraid if I caught a numb foot on a submerged log and had to dive under the ice again, I might not have the strength to get back to the surface.

I kept my eye on the prize—the shoreline. I don't know how long it took but eventually I reached ice solid enough to support me. With my snowshoes as a handhold, I pulled myself onto my elbows, leaned way out over the ice, kicked from below and rolled onto the ice.

I was out of the water. But I wasn't out of the woods.

I was face down about 10 feet from the tree line, my fingers still clutching the snowshoes, my chin in the snow, panting like a dog.

I might have been cursing my wool pants and shirt when I was in the water because of the weight they added, but now that I was out of the water, I was grateful for my Johnson woolies. Unlike cotton and other fabrics, wool keeps you warm even when wet. If you don't believe me, ask a sheep.

I was numb with cold. My fingers were wrapped so tight through the snowshoe webbing it was like they were glued. So, I used the Tubbs' tails as a crutch. I jammed the tail of each snowshoe

into the ice in front of me and pulled myself
up to my knees. I paused, took a few more
deep breaths, gritted my teeth and managed
to get both heavy feet beneath me. I staggered
over to the safety of the tree line dragging my
snowshoes with me.

I had no intention of taking time to start a fire.
I had a few hours of daylight left. If I could just
get back to my truck, I would have plenty of heat
once I fired it up.

I shook myself like a good water dog as Torro
had shown me how to do many times. Then,
I crossed my arms and jammed my hands into
my shirt and under my armpits to warm them.
I danced a wobbly jig for a count of 50 to get my
blood moving again.

As soon as I had a little feeling back in my
fingers, I found a downed tree, sat and untied
each boot and emptied them out. I wrung the
water out of my socks and put them back on. I
wasn't asking for dry. I just wanted to carry less
weight walking out.

I grabbed my snowshoes and strapped the
bindings back onto my boots as best I could with
fingers made clumsy from the cold. I walked
over to an inch-thick sapling and broke it off
to use as a walking stick. Then I headed back

as fast as I could go—this time sticking to the safety of the trees until I made it back to my tracks atop the frozen stream bed.

My clothes were pretty stiff by the time I got back to the truck an hour and a half later. When I bent down to kick the leather bindings off my boots, thin sheets of ice fell from the back of my coat and pant legs. I placed the snowshoes in the truck bed and dug my hand into my pants pockets. I hadn't even thought to check for the truck key earlier. I was some relieved to find it still in my pocket. I swiped it across my palm to dry it off and managed to unlock the door.

I slid into the truck cab. For some reason my hand began shaking like I had stuck my finger in an electric outlet when I reached for the ignition with the key. Maybe it was the anticipation of being warm soon. When the engine fired up, it was among the sweetest sounds I'd ever heard.

I pawed around the cab and found a dry pair of mittens and an old knit cap. I put them on while I waited for the truck engine to warm up. I jigged my knees and kept curling and uncurling my toes while I waited.

As soon as I had some feeling in my legs, I

shifted the truck into drive and headed out. I threw the heat on full blast in the cab, pulled off a mitten and jammed my fingers down the throat of the heating vent.

The hotter the heat blew, the more I shivered. Worse, my clothes were so wet the windshield fogged up like I was boiling potatoes in the front seat. I used my mitten to wipe down the dripping windshield, rolled my driver's window down and kept driving with the heat on full.

It was a half hour ride to my home. The wife and kids were away visiting relatives down country. I had the place to myself. Good thing. They worried enough about me.

I kicked off my sodden boots just inside the house door and shuffled to the shower on feet that felt like pine slabs.

After the longest, hottest shower of my life, I put on some long johns and two pairs of heavy socks. Then I ran into our bedroom, pulled a few blankets out of the cedar chest and headed for the smoldering wood stove in the living room. I tossed the blankets on the big overstuffed chair closest to the wood stove. I opened the stove damper to let the smoke rise, popped the door open and tossed chunks of maple and ash on the fire. I knew I should shut the stove door to get the most heat, but I wanted to see the flames.

I poured myself a shot of whiskey, walked back to the recliner and set my shot glass down on the corner of an end table piled high with books, magazines and papers. I wrapped the blankets around me like a papoose and sat down with my feet on the ottoman in front of the firebox.

I reached for my glass. My blanketed elbow triggered an avalanche of paper spilling onto my lap. A photo caught my eye. I held it up to the firelight.

It was a photo of Torro and me. I was leaning my backside against the tailgate of my old Chevy truck. My shotgun was across my lap and Torro was sitting beside me, leaning right into me. There was a good day's take of waterfowl surrounding us. We both had big grins on our faces.

I hadn't seen that photo in years. The wife must have found it and slid it into a "you gotta do something with this stuff" pile.

What were the odds of that photo falling into my lap right after I'd clawed my way out of that icy beaver marsh the way Torro had taught me to do?

I picked up my whiskey glass and raised a toast to Torro.

The next morning, I headed into town, had the photo scanned, printed up big and framed.

It hangs above my desk, with the rest of my family.

"I saw the bed of the truck start to rock back and forth—first gently and then like someone was shaking a can of rocks. I heard booming sounds, like a horse kicking a stall door."

TOO LOOSE MOOSE

Vermont's game wardens had a lot of trouble with moose when they began returning to Vermont in the late 1970s.

Moose were native to Vermont but had been extirpated—a fancy word which means they were native to the state but we killed them all. No one had seen a moose traipsing Vermont's woods for generations.

But thanks to conservation efforts throughout northern New England, moose numbers were on the upswing in a big way. Maine and New Hampshire's moose numbers had grown so much limited hunting seasons were being established.

Here in the Green Mountains, we knew it was only a matter of time until a moose from the Granite State swam the Connecticut River—or skated across it in winter and adopted Vermont as his home.

Their pattern of moving into new territory is

pretty well documented. Younger males come first—driven out by the older, more dominant bulls. The female moose, called cows, generally stay behind with the bigger, stronger, dominant bulls. As the herds grew and the bigger bulls and cows needed more forage, they followed.

The problem was the early pioneers often were lonely, especially in the fall when their hormones kicked in big time. These bachelor moose went looking for female company. Unable to locate cows of their own species, some looked about the Vermont landscape for the next best thing and went goofy for dairy cows.

It might be cute for the tourists, and down in Rutland County someone even turned a love struck moose-heifer romance into a kid's book, but it was no joke for dairy farmers to have a moose loitering nearby. Escorting the cows from the pasture into the barn for milking twice a day when a big bull moose believes those cows are his girlfriends can get you killed.

It was the game wardens' job to keep the moose and humans from hurting each other. We didn't want to kill the young bulls. We wanted them here. With luck, they would eventually find female moose and our moose population would grow. At the same time, we could not let any moose hurt people.

It was a balancing act.

I first heard about a young bull moose wandering around Elmore in July. It was good news. We all kept it kind of quiet among ourselves and hoped the youngster would stay out of the public eye.

But it was not to be. Before long I got word he was cozying up to the cows on a dairy farm.

When Ernie went down to bring the cows in for milking, the gangly moose would trail along behind his black and white girlfriends, hanging back 100 feet or more and just watching.

At first, it was just cute. He wasn't causing any problems.

But as the days grew shorter and the season changed, the young moose started to get more protective of what he now perceived to be his harem. His hormone levels were rising. The rut—mating season was coming.

In the world of moose, size matters. A lot. From the bull moose's perspective, to have to stand back and watch some creature the size of a month old moose calf, with only two legs, no antlers, swinging a tiny stick in his hoof, try to steal your girls away from you is pretty insulting.

The bachelor bull started to get more aggressive when Ernie went to collect his cows. The bull lowered his antlers, his neck muscles swelled, he blew out and pawed the ground.

Ernie had a master's degree in bovine language and it appeared to be very similar to wild moose. He realized his days of walking down into the pasture and escorting his cows in for twice daily milking were numbered if he didn't act.

Being a conservation-conscious fellow and not wanting to kill the moose, he decided to make himself appear to be a bigger challenger. Ernie wrapped himself in some serious farmer armor.

He climbed up into the cab of his biggest tractor—a dual axle John Deere diesel with a cab and front bucket. The moose would have to be a real moron to charge that, he figured.

Ernie's cows associated all farm machinery with humans and humans with food. So the girls weren't bothered by the tractor rumbling through their pasture and blowing smoke. They followed along.

The moose backed off when the engine roared and the black smoke poured from the exhaust pipe. Ernie was able to get the cows out of the pasture and into the milking parlor.

"Brilliant!" as the Brits say.

For a couple days anyway.

The bull's testosterone levels were still rising. He was programmed to fight for the right to keep his cows. After awhile it didn't matter that the big green monster looked nothing like a moose or even that a fight with it would probably be a losing battle. Mother Nature told the young bull he needed to fight to keep his females or die trying.

Crazed by hormones, the bull started charging the tractor.

Ernie had had enough. He gave me a call.

We all knew the best solution for our confused cow suitor was for us to find him a girlfriend of his own species. But there just weren't any to be found in this neighborhood.

So, I gave my friend and fellow warden, John, a call. John and I decided the best thing to do was to tranquilize the bull and haul him up to the Hurricane Wildlife Management Area in Norton, a two-hour drive away.

Department biologists advised there was a small population of moose already established in that area. Our hope was that once we got this bull moose looking at his own kind, he would give up courting dairy cows.

A little ride was in order.

John knew another farmer, Charlie, who was skilled in tranquilizing hard-to-catch heifers. I gave Charlie a call to see if he would be willing to help John and I move this moose. Charlie considered it an interesting proposition. We three decided to meet the next morning at Ernie's, after the morning milking but before the afternoon milking, so the moose would be in his least agitated mood.

I then gave Harold a call. Harold picked up downed livestock from local farmers with a truck set up just for that purpose. It had nice ramp, high oak side racks, and a winch. Unlike many metal cattle trailers, it did not have a roof on it. I thought Harold's truck would be safer for our moose and for us to get out of in case of an emergency. Harold said he was game too.

The next day brought bright sun, a little bite in the air and light frost on the ground. We were all assembled at the edge of the pasture by 9 am. Harold and John and Charlie and I, along with Ernie and his family, stood on the outside of the fence a safe distance up near the barn looking down into the cows. Towering at the back of the herd was our suitor.

For the moment at least, the bull was standing contentedly. He didn't seem too concerned about us.

Charlie turned to me to ask how much tranquilizer to draw up to give a bull moose.

I didn't have a clue, and said so. Charlie and John and Ernie and I talked it over and decided Charlie ought to draw up a dose big enough to drop a 700 pound cow. That would be a good place to start, we thought. We didn't want to give the bull so much it would kill him. We thought it better to err on the side of caution. We wanted the moose down, but not dead.

Charlie had a nicely organized zippered kit from which he lifted a vial and a dart. He drew the liquid into the syringe as skilled as any nurse. He placed the vial—which was still better than half full—back inside the kit, zipped it shut and tucked the kit inside his jacket.

He loaded the darted syringe into a 20-gauge shotgun, took a look through the scope to make certain it was clear, nodded to me, and said he was ready to go.

"Okay, let's try this," I said. We circled around the

side of the pasture, through the brush, with the intent of keeping the beast as close as we could to the barnyard. John stayed with Harold and Ernie. John would send Harold and the truck down once the moose dropped from the drug.

In addition to Charlie's dart gun, I carried a rifle over my shoulder as well as my pistol at my side. We stayed a good 150 feet away from our moose, moved quietly, and spoke only in whispers. We did not want the moose to consider us a threat. If he charged us I might have little choice but to kill him.

But the lovesick moose was entirely focused on his girlfriends. He didn't even turn his head to look our way, although I am certain he saw us. Having seen humans working on the farm daily made it easy for us. For now anyway, as long we didn't try to take his females, he would tolerate our presence.

I stopped about 100 feet from the bull, still outside the pasture fence, looked at Charlie and whispered, "How close do you need to be for your shot?" I knew the syringe was going to fly slower and wobblier than a bullet.

"Closer the better," he said.

"Well, he's behaving right now," I replied. "Okay,

let's go in a bit closer and hope he stays calm. You go first. If he charges, you run. I'll cover you."

Charlie stepped forward, out to the right and a little in front of me. About 75 feet from the bull, Charlie dropped to a knee, focused his scope, took a long breath, paused and pulled the trigger.

The dart flew and slammed into the bull's behind, just as we planned.

The moose shuddered and took a step sideways as if stung by a bee. Then he stopped, turned and looked at his backside, where the dart hung. Unable to reach and knock it loose with his head, he shrugged his shoulders and turned to look ahead placidly once again.

"Nice shot!" I whispered to Charlie.

"Thanks," he said.

We remained crouched and waited for the bull to collapse like on all those Wild Kingdom episodes. We waited. And waited.

Nothing. The moose just continued to stand there. The dart still clung in the moose's hairy behind. My legs began to cramp up. I dropped to one knee.

"How long is it supposed to take?" I asked Charlie after a minute or so.

"Not this long," he said.

We gave it another few minutes. The bull's expression didn't change. His head didn't lower and his knees did not buckle. He just stood there among the cows and flicked an ear to shake off a fly every once in awhile.

"I guess we'd better try a second dose," Charlie said.

"Okay," I said.

We agreed to go with a second syringe load that would immobilize a horse, which according to Charlie was about double the amount he used to drop a cow to its knees.

This moose might look mellow, but he apparently required enough tranquilizer to knock down an elephant.

Charlie put his shotgun down, sat back on his haunches and pulled the zippered kit from inside his jacket and loaded up a second dart.

Then he rocked himself forward onto his knees, shuffled a bit, sat back, steadied himself and fired. The second dart also went into the moose's flank, a few inches above the first dart. Now the bull was sporting two darts in his rump.

The bull decided whatever bugs were biting, he had had enough of them. His head went up, he leaned back and took several big steps forward. The cows in front of him scattered like chickens.

He was on the move, headed towards the woods. I guess he figured these nasty biting bugs would leave him alone there.

I winced. Charlie grimaced.

We knew if he made it into the woods there would be no way for Harold to drive his truck through the trees to the downed moose. It would be impossible to load the bull and transport him to his new home.

We had to stop the moose before he got into the trees.

I heard some yelling off behind me. It was John. He was running down the hill from the other side of the pasture and motioning to me.

I read John's mind. If we could turn the moose and keep him from entering the woods, keep him in the pasture, we would have a chance to get him. Charlie and I jumped through the fence and into the pasture, running and hollering and waving our arms from below the moose, trying to startle and turn him. John was coming at us from the other side, doing the same, with Ernie following.

We were betting our lives on that double dose of tranquilizer. If the moose decided to charge instead of run, we could be run over, maybe gored. Those antlers weren't just for decoration.

If the bull had not been drugged, we would never have outmaneuvered him. Moose can run faster than a horse for short distances.

I don't know if the yelling had an effect or it was just the tranquilizer. But the moose slowed his trot to the woods like a wind up toy needing to be wound. His head lowered, his legs wobbled. About 75 feet from the tree line, he stopped.

The four of us froze in our tracks, waiting to see what the moose would do next.

We stared and waited. The bull should collapse any second now. I watched as he swayed back and forth, his antlers rocking. I saw the darts fall at last from his hairy hip.

His head dropped below his knees. Any minute now he should collapse like a bad soufflé. John motioned to me and we started walking closer, convinced the moose was going down.

But our movements set him off again. He threw up his head, dug in his heels and pushed off, propelling himself forward like a battered football player determined to cross the goal line.

Now what?

John shouted, "Eric, fire your gun!" John and I drew our pistols and started shooting up into the air like cowboys turning a herd of Texas Longhorns.

The shots startled and confused the moose. He stopped fast, stumbled and his nose touched the ground. His rear legs were rocking, but he had locked his front knees like a horse taking a nap. His eyes were glazed. But it did not appear he was ever going to collapse.

I walked over to John and said, "Now what do we do?"

"I guess we gotta go get him," John said.

John holstered his pistol and waved to Harold at the top of the hill. Harold jumped in the cab and entered the pasture.

John had brought a good length of nylon

rope with him. He made a big lasso and we approached the moose—not head on, but from an angle. I had my rifle at the ready in case the moose charged. We were maybe 10 feet from the moose and his antlers were just a few feet from the ground. John gave the rope a toss. He missed, but the moose stood as still as a weeping willow in a light summer breeze. He was swaying just a little.

It took John two more tosses to get the rope around the bull's antlers. He pulled it taut and played out more line. Harold had arrived with his truck. He backed up slowly towards the moose and stopped it 10 feet from his nose. The moose was as quiet as a 1,000 pound puppy.

Now what do we do?

Harold climbed out of the truck cab and seeing as how he and Charlie and Ernie were the cow moving experts, I deferred to them.

All three said it would be best to pull the moose down to the ground, roll him onto his side, then slide him up the ramp into the truck bed.

I looked at the moose towering above me, his eyes glazed, his mouth slightly open and drooling, and hoped he remained comatose throughut this procedure.

Harold, Charlie and Ernie all stood behind
John and pulled together on the rope, now tight
around the bull's antlers. I stood a few feet back
and to the side in case I had to tip him one way
or the other, or grab my pistol.

Our cattlemen knew their stuff. The moose
unlocked his knees and crumpled down into
a nice, neat long-legged heap. Harold lowered
the truck gate and grabbed the winch cable. He
placed the hook over a second rope that John
had placed around the bull's neck. It was a
knotted loop that served as a collar, tied so the
knot would not slide and choke him.

With the remote in his hand, Harold activated
the cable.

The moose's head came up, and with John on
one side and me on the other, we helped direct
the big brown head up the ramp so the antlers
would not get caught as the beast slowly slid up
onto the ramp.

Halfway up the ramp, Harold stopped towing
and John and I looked at each other, a bit
puzzled.

"Gotta hog tie those feet. You don't want him
standing up until you get to where you are
going," Charlie said to me.

"Oh! Good idea," I said.

This was my first moose round up.

John and I had brought plenty of rope. I cut some up and set to work pulling those long legs together and securing them with Ernie and John's help.

Harold and Ernie and Charlie looked over my work. Harold tied the final bow and he left a big tail on it. I must have looked a little puzzled.

"You want to be able to pull this line here and free the moose when you are ready. You don't want to have to get in there with him flailing his legs around and maybe lose your head."

Smart! I was learning a lot.

Then Harold hit the button on the remote once again and the bull slid easily into the truck bed. You could kill or seriously injure many animals using their neck to move them like this. But moose have tremendously strong necks. We knew the young bull would not be hurt.

We got our moose loaded and breathed a big sigh of relief.

John jumped into the truck bed and tied the

moose's antlers to the corner post at the front of the truck rack. I pinched an aluminum tag onto the bull's ear, so the Department could identify him in the future if he ever showed up again. Lastly, we ran the hog tie rope out the bottom of the truck bed rack so we could tug on it and free his feet when we got to Norton. We were ready to roll.

It was then I thought to ask Charlie a question.

"Hey Charlie, how long before this stuff wears off?"

"Generally, lasts about an hour or so," Charlie said.

"Holy cow," I shouted. "We gotta go! It's a two-hour ride to the Hurricane."

Harold jumped into the driver's seat and John dove for the passenger seat in the truck. I ran up the hill. By the time Harold's truck was lumbering out of the pasture, I was in my cruiser, ready to follow.

All went well for about 50 minutes into the ride, until we were just outside of Island Pond.

I saw the bed of the truck start to rock back and forth—first gently and then like someone was shaking a can of rocks.

185

BOOM! BOOM!

It sounded like a horse kicking a stall door.

Oh my.

I sped up to get closer to the truck for a better look. I saw two big, brown hairy humps peeking out over the top of the eight-foot side racks—they were the unmistakable shoulders of a large, angry moose.

"Good God, the beast is standing up," I thought.

The shoulders were soon followed by a wobbly antler waving up above the top of the truck cab.

Another few miles and both antlers were visible. They about filled the entire width of the truck bed.

Another mile or two and there was a big brown nose and twitching ears.

Was he enjoying the scenery? Looking for his harem? Getting ready to make a break for it?

I noticed John leaning half way out the passenger side door of the truck. He was twisted back around trying to get a look at what was going on up above the cab.

John and I were a good team. I figured he was thinking what I was thinking, which was: If that moose figured out how to climb those wooden racks, it could spell disaster not just for the moose, but for any drivers on the road—for instance, me—following behind.

John disappeared back inside the cab. A few seconds later I saw the truck begin swerving like a snake back and forth across the road. I dropped back to watch.

Harold hit the brakes and sped up again. He did this a couple times. I knew he was trying to knock the moose off his feet.

The truck became a bucking horse. The moose was the cowboy.

Apparently, our moose was a budding rodeo star. He might still be under the influence, but he refused to be knocked down again.

So much for my hog tie.

Our only hope was the rope John had tied around his antlers and fastened to that stout corner post before we headed out. It was the only thing holding him down now.

Seeing that evasive action was not going to work,

Harold signaled that he was pulling off to the right. I followed and braked hard, kicking up a cloud of dust.

I jumped out of the cruiser and climbed up on the side of the truck bed to take a look at the rope securing the bull's antlers, while John jumped up on the rear bumper and leaned over the ramp.

I saw the antler rope was still knotted well and was debating as to whether to stick my hand in there and try to do more with the rope when I heard a BLAM.

The truck bed rocked and I grabbed on for dear life and looked behind me.

The bull had spotted John coming up behind him and kicked out hard, smashing his dinner plate sized hoof against the tailgate, just inches from John's head. Clearly, our moose was no longer sedated.

John dropped back down to land on the bumper, grinned and shook his head. His ears were probably ringing.

Harold and Ernie and I conferred for about five seconds. The consensus was we just had to keep going and pray.

We drove through Island Pond with the truck rocking and the moose banging and people stopping and turning to stare at the big brown nose and antlers weaving above the side racks.

Another 45 minutes passed with the moose thrashing, banging, stomping, and me gritting my teeth and praying. Finally, Harold pulled into the wildlife management area.

As soon as the truck stopped, all three of us jumped out, expecting to witness one heck of a racket. But it was quiet inside the truck bed.

The moose had calmed down. Maybe he was exhausted from thrashing. Maybe he was carsick. Maybe he was hung over. Maybe he decided he liked seeing the state this way. We will never know.

The three of us made a point of not slamming our doors when we got out. We whispered our release plan. It was agreed I would cut the rope free from our boy's antlers as soon as John and Harold lowered the tailgate.

Harold and John unlatched the ramp locks and lowered it to the ground as quietly as they could.

While the bull's eyes focused on the commotion behind him, I cut his antlers free of the rope and leaned back just in case he wanted to swipe me with his rack before he backed out.

John and Harold dove for the safety of the truck fenders.

We waited for a clatter of big hooves and the sight of a moose heading into the Hurricane.

It didn't happen. There was no Disney movie dive for freedom.

Maybe he smelled a bigger moose out there and was scared. Maybe he hoped he'd bought a round trip ticket. He just stood there.

"Rattle the front rack," Harold told John and me. That did it. The moose came to life fast. Startled, he threw his nose into the air, spun around, took one big leap off the tailgate and pranced off towards the woods.

We figured he would dash into the brush and disappear.

But not this Romeo. He was used to people. He wandered off slowly, pausing to nip a few aspen twigs on his way. He stopped about 80 feet away and turned to look back at us.

"Let's get this ramp up before he runs back in," John joked.

Harold and I chuckled and the three of us closed the truck ramp.

I thanked Harold for his capable assistance. He said he'd enjoyed it. We told him to send us the bill, which we would forward to the Department.

Then John and I jumped in my cruiser and I drove the two plus hours back to base.

I gave Ernie and Charlie each a quick call to let them know we had released the moose safely and to thank them for their help too.

The next morning I called the wardens working the Norton area to let them know there was a new young bull in their neck of the woods.

I gave them a general description and told them about the tag and his past history of bonding with bovines.

I thought sure I'd heard the last of him.

But about three weeks later, my colleague, Roger, from up in the wilds of Holland, called me to say he had a complaint from a dairy farmer there.

"Hey, Eric. There's a young bull moose up here that's moved in with some heifers. He's being quite a nuisance," Roger said. "I think it's your moose."

I listened carefully. What were the odds it was the same moose we had dropped off a good 10 miles or more away several weeks ago.

"Has he got a tag in his ear?" I asked Roger.

"I drove out and took a good look at him this morning," Roger said.

He was keeping me in suspense. I could hear his big grin right through the phone line.

"Yup. This youngster is sporting a shiny new silver earring."

Dang. No question it was our moose.

I stood there in silence, trying to come up with an appropriate response.

Roger piped back up, "Hey, Eric, come get your moose!"

That bull would be stew meat first, I thought to myself.

Finally I said, "Roger, you remember 'Finders Keepers' when you were a kid? I think that's sorta the kinda situation we have here.

You do whatever you want with that Romeo. He's all yours."

Roger laughed.

I sure was happy when the cows came over the mountain—cow moose that is.

"And then all that stuff that went
down, it all came up. A plume of
muddy water, smoke, meat, maggots,
flies, bone, fur and some pretty
shocked looking fish. Their mouths
were wide open just like mine."

Moose Vesuvius

How do you remove a rotting moose carcass stuck deep in the mud?

Part of a warden's job is occasionally dealing with really gross stuff, so this topic was a good one. Any tips from fellow wardens were most appreciated, especially if it was shared over some homemade wine in the light of a campfire after a long day of work, as this tale was.

I was attending a conference up in Maine with a bunch of other wildlife officials. After work it was common for us all to gather around a campfire, sip a little adult beverage and swap stories. And that's where I was now holding a cup of dandelion wine.

Brownie had the floor. He was a good storyteller and we all liked him. I leaned in to listen. He launched into a story about a big dead moose that was stinking up the neighborhood something awful in his patrol area—which was most of northern Maine.

One thinks of a pristine pond and imagines chirping birds, green buds, the call of loons, jumping trout, and sweet mountain air. Brownie said all of that lovely tourist photo stuff was there, except the sweet mountain air part.

The odor on the breeze from the rotting moose carcass at the edge of that pond was dead-mouse-in-your-truck-air-ducts times ten, gag and run bad, he said.

Anyone who has had a mouse die and decompose in their car knows it can take weeks or even months for the stench to disappear. Compare the body mass of a miniscule mouse to a massive moose and you begin to understand the magnitude of the stench.

The city people were arriving to open up their camps for the summer. The smell was so bad they couldn't go outside or open their windows. Depending on which way the wind was blowing, some would not even want to leave their cars. There wasn't a hardware store within 20 miles that had enough air freshener to mask the stink.

Brownie was called in to investigate. As he

told the story, he canoed around the perimeter and it wasn't hard to find the problem—a big bull moose made twice as big due to the blow flies that were feeding on his remains—down and dead in a critical feeder stream leading into this previously pristine pond. Whether the deceased had broken through winter ice and been unable to get out, died of natural or man-made causes, it was too late to know or care.

Brownie told his rapt audience that he first tried the cowboy approach, with a red bandana over his nose and mouth to keep from gulping down blow flies and to hide his gagging from anyone who might be on shore with a video camera or binoculars. When the wind came full into his face, it was a god awful stench even for a seasoned outdoorsman like himself.

He made a lariat and tossed it up and over an antler from his canoe. It took a couple tries, but he was successful. He tied the line around the front seat of his canoe and laid the line carefully so it would play out over the gunwale as he paddled backwards, to give himself some distance and leverage.

In about 30 feet, the line was played out and taut. Brownie dug his paddle in and pulled at the water. His pirogue slammed to a halt with his hemp rope tuned to high E. That carcass would not budge.

He tried the old triangle approach, seesawing his craft from side to side and even sticking his paddle into the muddy bottom to get more purchase on the rope and free up the remains. No go. The big antlers rocked a bit as if to taunt him and a hoof shook in the breeze, but the massive moose would not move.

Sweaty, thirsty, bit up by all manner of nasty gnats, flecked with pond scum and mud and more than a little put out, Brownie decided the answer had to be getting the moose outta there piece by piece.

But there was no meat saw in the canoe, no power cord to plug one into anyway. Brownie briefly considered a chainsaw. But there was no easy way to get close enough to use one of those either—without getting stuck yourself and maybe ending up like the moose—stuck and dead. An ax would be barbaric and take forever too.

What to do?

Brownie scanned our faces in the flickering firelight for dramatic pause. No one made a sound. We were enthralled like cub scouts listening to a good ghost story.

Satisfied he still had our full attention, Brownie took a sip of wine and then continued with his story.

He said he had to admit he was stumped. He canoed up to the carcass, untied his line and let it float in the water. Then he paddled back to a point where he could pull down his bandana and gulp fresh air, get some perspective on the matter and ponder.

They say necessity is the mother of invention and Brownie had necessity big time. He didn't want any more calls about this stinking moose.

Sitting there looking at the beast from a distance of 100 feet or so, Brownie thought about how badly stuck the remains were. "He's stuck in there like a boulder," he thought.

"Hmmmmmm. How do you get rid of a big rock?"

The answer came to him like a bolt from the blue: "Dynamite!"

Plus, he reasoned, it would be a heck of a lot

of fun and give him great personal satisfaction since he had been out there for a couple hours now, gagging, sweating, getting bug bit, and getting nowhere.

We were speechless at Brownie's brilliance. Dynamite! A murmur of approval ran through his audience. Big grins were seen in the firelight. We all squirmed in our seats eager to hear what happened next.

"Yes, gentlemen. Dynamite. I came back the next day with two sticks and bam. Problem solved. Moose gone!"

And with that, Brownie drained his glass, as did we all, shouting out praise and applauding.

We congratulated Brownie for his ingenious solution. I sat there a bit envious imagining the sense of victory Brownie must have felt and the fun of seeing that dynamite blow.

I filed the story away in my memory bank. I doubted I would ever get the chance to try his method. At the time, Maine's moose population was booming, but Vermont's was only getting started. And what were the odds of a moose dropping dead in a pond anyhow?

Still, what a stroke of genius. And what fun!
You learn a lot at these conferences.

Years passed when out of the blue I got a
call from our dispatcher that fishermen were
complaining about a dead cow moose stinking
up pretty Little Elmore pond.

Reports were that it was smelling pretty bad and
that canoeists and kayakers were complaining
about the stink. I should get it out of there before
the calls got worse along with the heat of summer.

Little Elmore is a jewel of a pond, tucked
between Mount Elmore and Route 12, about
a half-mile hike from the nearest road. To
get that dead moose outta there and load it
into my pickup truck bed and haul it to the
Department's dead deer pit would not be fun.
Even if I towed it to shore with the canoe.

I would have to drag it somewhere and bury it
or cover it up really well to stop the stench of
decay. That was a job for a backhoe, not one
guy with a shovel. Any which way I looked at
this job, it was going to be a lot of work.

It was then I remembered the campfire back in
Maine and Brownie's story about the dynamite.
Could this be my chance?

With the realization I had a situation just like Brownie, a really unpleasant job turned into a gift from above.

I got on the radio, trying to hide my schoolboy glee, and called my neighboring warden, Ron. I knew Ron had relatives who worked in construction and demolition. I calmly proposed dynamiting a moose carcass, as if it was no big deal and we did this every day.

What did he think? Would he like to be there?

Just as I had hoped, Ron was similarly up to the challenge. In fact, I heard him clear his throat a couple times as he tried to respond in a steady, manly-voiced tone instead of that of a 16 year-old boy about to get the keys to dad's car. I got it. I could barely contain my glee too.

Ron said not only would he help, he would bring the dynamite, caps and fuse wire too. How much did we need?

I didn't have a clue. But I couldn't tell Ron that.

I put my brain in overdrive trying to remember the details of Brownie's inspirational story. But as I pondered, I realized Brownie's tale was big on drama, but very thin on the specifics.

Darn.

There was silence and static on the radio as I drove and thought, until Ron came back and said, "Eric? You still there? Over."

I knew I had to come up with some sort of number and act as though I knew what I was talking about or I might blow this rare opportunity to blow up a moose.

So, I pushed the talk button and said—with all the seasoned voice of experience I could fake, "Oh, I think two sticks should do it. Over."

I guess Ron didn't notice the hesitation in my voice and just thought I had landed in a dead zone for a few seconds.

"Roger," he said.

We agreed to meet at the Little Elmore fishing access early the next morning. Ron would bring the dynamite and I would bring the canoe and rope.

I was as happy as a retriever pup bringing in her first bird. Truth be told, I had trouble sleeping that night just thinking about the next morning's adventure.

If I had joined the Department a few years earlier, I would have been able to obtain dynamite as part of the job. Wardens used to routinely sign out a few sticks to remove pesky beaver dams in an expeditious manner for frustrated property owners.

Sadly, our easy access to dynamite had ended several years before I became part of the force.

Legend has it the policy change was the result of a few wardens who forgot that water runs downhill. They blew up some beaver dams and town roads were washed out. That stirred up a few road commissioners who had to find the money to fix the roads.

Or maybe the Department just knew guys like me were coming up the ranks. I don't know for sure.

As promised, Ron met me bright and early the next morning at the portage point with two sticks of dynamite and an equal number of blasting caps. Just one problem, he said. His uncle could only come up with 35 feet of fuse wire.

Was that enough fuse, Ron asked?

I had no idea, but I wasn't about to tell Ron that.

Brownie never mentioned how far away he had

been before he touched off the dynamite. Heck, I wasn't really sure how long 35 feet was even. I'm no carpenter. How far is home plate to the pitcher's mound? Sixty feet? So this is half of that plus five feet? Hmmmmm.

My mind started to work on all the maxims I could recall from years of schooling.

"One if by land, two if by sea." This was a pond. There were two of us and one moose. The numbers worked, but that was about all.

"Don't shoot until you see the whites of their eyes." Moose is already dead. Not a good fit either.

"The square root of a hypotenuse is..." Never could remember that one. And we would be in a straight line from the carcass anyway.

Shucks.

Ron stood quietly, waiting for my answer.

I looked down at my boots and hoped Ron didn't notice the ice growing inside. I felt a big case of cold feet coming on.

I shook off my doubts, with thoughts of Brownie and how magnificent his story was.

I decided we just had to go for it.

"Yeah, that should be plenty of fuse," I said, like I knew what I was talking about.

I breathed a big silent sigh of relief when Ron turned his back to grab the rest of his gear. Ron believed I knew what I was doing.

Good.

I was as happy as a six year old reaching for a plate of freshly baked chocolate chip cookies at grandma's house—where you can have as many as you want. This was gonna be fun!

I leaned over the side of the pickup bed and lifted up the bow of my canoe. Ron grabbed the stern. "Wow. This canoe is light," he said. "We both gonna fit in this?"

I had brought my super light, one-man racing canoe for this task, figuring we could both squeeze in it, but that it would lessen the weight of the portage and get us closer to the carcass if the beast was stuck in the mud like Brownie's had been.

"I want to be able to get right next to the moose and not get stuck," I said. "It's a little tight for two of us, but we'll be all right. Plus, it's a lot easier to carry in." I didn't mention how tippy it was. Ron would figure that out soon enough.

I grabbed my duffle bag and opened it. "Want to put the dynamite in here?" I asked him.

"Yup, that's good," he said, and in went the two sticks. Then he put the blasting caps in his right breast shirt pocket, the battery in the left, and the fuse wire he tucked into a pants pocket. We were all set.

I grinned at Ron. Ron grinned at me. We were off.

The portage in went fast and smooth and we didn't break a sweat in the cool air. A couple of red squirrels chattered at us. That was all. At the shoreline the fog was still settled on the center of the pond. I unzipped my duffle and picked up my binoculars and scanned the shoreline.

I quickly spied our horizontal host. It was a big, very bloated cow floating maybe 200 yards from shore near the quiet north end of the pond. She looked like a flopped Adirondack guide boat with legs. A nice hatch of flies was swarming around her, too. Those flies would attract fish and that could mean some nice trout for dinner as a bonus.

"Eric," Ron said, interrupting my reverie. "Didn't you tell me this moose was stuck in the mud?

Does it matter that she's just floating out there?"

Hunh. I had no idea whether it made any difference if our target was out in the pond floating rather than in the mud as in Brownie's story. But again, I didn't want to concern Ron. So, I said, "Well, Ron, no one actually said where this moose was. Brownie's moose was stuck in the mud, so I just assumed this one was. But I don't think it makes any difference."

And just to reassure Ron a bit more, I added, "Actually, it looks like we have it a lot easier than Brownie. We don't have to canoe into a marsh and risk getting stuck. We can paddle right up to her."

Ron nodded like I was making sense. I believed it myself.

A light early morning breeze was at our backs as we pushed off. Ron got in first, as we agreed I had the most experience with this canoe, so I should be at the stern. It was cramped, but we quickly got our balance and as long as we didn't move an inch we felt safe. If I had known the cow was drifting with the breeze, I would have chosen a bigger, more stable canoe.

Fog swirled around the moose carcass along with clouds of flies as the sun began to heat up the water. Fish were jumping. It was a lovely quiet morning, which we intended to interrupt in a very big way, very soon.

Because it was Ron's relative's dynamite and because it was my canoe and because we were cramped like sardines, I decided Ron should have the honor of stuffing the dynamite and caps inside the carcass, running out the fuse and touching off the charges.

I would focus on keeping us on top of the water.

In retrospect, I am not sure giving Ron the job of poking dynamite into the maggoty guts of a putrid moose corpse was much of an honor, but being a good sport Ron accepted the job without a word of complaint.

We paddled forward and the stench grew as we approached.

The fish, which had been rising around the

carcass, grew fewer in number, although the clouds of flies remained.

As we got closer, it seemed to me I didn't have to paddle towards the cow so much as try and stay out of her way. Maybe there were currents in the pond or maybe her bloated belly acted as a sail, catching the slightest wind and delicately moving her like a giant water bug in the breeze. Maybe both. But it almost looked like the dead moose was sailing over to meet us.

Ron and I slowed our progression. I turned the bow and paddled us right next to the cow's big bloated belly. Ron and I drifted past the big head, over a front hoof and ducked beneath a stiff front leg. I was grateful for the calm water. In a stiff breeze, there would be a chance her body could flip and we would be tossed into the pond.

I watched Ron hunch forward, elbows at his side. He was busily putting the charges together in his lap, rocking our canoe.

"Ron, how you doing up there? You ready?"

"I just gotta get my knife," Ron said, bending forward to reach for a knife at his feet. That little move tipped our canoe and nearly knocked us over. "Whoa!" I yelped, plunging my paddle deep into the water to keep us steady.

"Sorry," Ron said. "But I'm going to have to cut her open and move a bit to get these charges into her. So get ready for more movement. How about one charge up between the ribs and the other way in the back?"

"Sounds good to me," I said. "Just let me know if I need to get you closer. The breeze is starting to pick up a little."

I paddled Ron in closer to the carcass. We were both wincing from the stink and the flies swarming in our eyes and ears. Ron used his knife to cut openings in the moose and smoothly inserted the two sticks and caps.

"Okay, they're in. Back up slowly," he said.

I paddled slowly in reverse as Ron let the fuse wire slide through his fingers, like a four-weight fly rod line. It didn't take long for the fuse to end. Not long at all. About four strokes in reverse and Ron said, "Okay then. That's it, Eric. Stop."

"That's it?" I asked with more than a little concern in my voice. Oh my. I could still see the swarms of flies on the carcass. In fact, I could count them.

"Yeah, that's the end of the fuse. Thirty-five feet like I told you," Ron said. "You said it would be enough. We're okay here, right?"

Thank heavens Ron could not turn around and look at me for fear of dumping us both in the pond. He would have seen the blood drain from my face and the look of terror in my eyes.

I swallowed hard and a shiver went down my spine—the kind you get when you think you might die and should have the good sense to make another choice.

I again tried to conjure up in my mind what, if anything, Brownie might have said about how much fuse he had used. Blowing up a moose had seemed so simple when Brownie told the story at the campfire.

Now, here Ron and I were seconds away from touching off two sticks of dynamite within spitting distance of our canoe and I had no idea if we would make it back to shore in one piece.

My only comfort was that I was three or four feet farther away from the dynamite charge than Ron, because I was in the stern. That meant he was 35 feet away and I was maybe 38 or 39 feet back from the charges.

I really didn't think the extra couple of feet would make much of a difference in my survival when the dynamite went off. And I was thinking I should switch places with Ron. But I didn't want to scare him. We were so close to getting this job done. Then again, I wasn't looking forward to explaining this to my boss if something bad happened.

Ron's common sense was kicking in too. He probably sensed my hesitation. Even though his back was to me, he said, "Geez, I wish we had a longer fuse." Yeah, me too, I said silently to myself. About 200 feet longer. Along with a much bigger boat, hard hats, safety goggles, and maybe a two-inch-thick Plexiglas wall to hide behind.

What was I thinking?

Oh well. We'd come this far. I decided there was no turning back. I took a deep breath and said in as confident an aw shucks-don't-worry voice as I could muster, "I think we'll will be all right."

And to make Ron feel more comfortable, I followed that with a factoid that might or might not matter from this distance. "Dynamite blows down, not sideways anyhow." Some old timer had told me that. I didn't know if that was really true either. Guess I was about to find out here pretty quick.

It was then I saw the fuse line was sagging a bit, which meant we had lost some distance. I realized the cow was drifting in towards us, because we were attached to her by an umbilical cord of dynamite and fuse wire.

That sent a big chill down my spine. It was as if this old cow moose was Moby Dick, chasing us.

Ron noticed the bloated beast closing in on us too and said, "Eric, she's getting closer. What do you want me to do?"

It was now or never. "Get ready, Ron. I am going to paddle us back here just enough to tighten the line. On the count of three, you touch 'er off," I said.

I angled the canoe so we were perpendicular to the putrid corpse and her fly posse. Then I stuck my paddle straight down into the water to brace the canoe and said, "Three."

Ron touched the battery to the fuse.

Ka-WHOOOOOOOOOOM!

Deafening.

The water in front of us parted in a deep dish shape. A hole deep enough to suck a dozen moose down to Davey Jones' locker appeared before us, like some sort of Biblical parting of the waters.

My mouth fell open. It was awesome.

And then all that stuff that went down, it all came up. A plume of muddy water, smoke, meat, maggots, flies, bone, fur and some pretty shocked looking fish. Their mouths were wide open just like mine.

We were in the middle of a volcanic eruption, our own mini Krakatoa. I braced for the tsunami. Ron and I hunkered down—our paddles fixed like outriggers on opposite sides of the canoe. My head sucked into my collar like a snapping turtle into his shell.

I shut my mouth and ducked.

A wall of water at least 10 feet high slammed into us, drenching and choking us. I doubt Little Elmore had ever seen waves that high. The canoe wasn't so much rocking as leaping. But all my white water training paid off. The canoe stayed upright—how, I don't know.

Then I heard something like hail hitting the
water, smacking me in the head, bouncing
off my shoulders and back and landing in
the canoe. Hail pings and stings. This was
different. I was being pummeled and smacked.

"What the ?"

I kept my head down and opened an eye. I saw
all different sizes of rocks, sticks, hide, moose
guts, pond bottom and I don't wanna know
raining down from the sky in a smoke brown
mist.

I held my breath and grabbed my paddle tight.

When the moose rain stopped and the water
began to calm I opened both my eyes. All
around us was a shimmering floating carpet
of greasy, stinking moose parts.

I looked at Ron's back and then down at my
lap. Ron had strands of something hanging
from his hat and sitting on his shirt back.
Our clothes were covered in an atomized soup
of moose intestines, hair, bone, pond weeds
and mud. Our green uniforms were mud
gray. It reminded me of photos I've seen of
the ash covered human remains found near
Mount Vesuvius, the volcano that blew its top

centuries ago in Italy. I don't want to belittle what happened there to those folks, but that's kind of what we looked like.

The good news for Ron and me was this slime had not hardened yet and we were still breathing.

My ears were ringing. If Ron was speaking to me, I couldn't hear him. I yelled to Ron and asked if he was okay. I saw Ron nod—maybe he was just finishing a prayer of thanks to God that he was still alive, I don't know. But the fact Ron was able to nod his head at all, in fact that he and I still had heads, was a huge relief to me.

What had I been thinking?

Ron, whether from shock or kindness or simply out of fear of tipping over the canoe, did not turn around and hit me with his fist or paddle, raise his voice or call me an idiot.

I started turning the canoe towards shore. I figured we were done.

That's when Ron saw it through the mist—the smoldering cow moose—one leg poking straight up in the air like an enemy flag flying from the mast. She refused to be sunk.

Two sticks of dynamite had done a lot of damage, but a goodly portion of her was still floating.

Ron shouted above the ringing in my ears, "Think we should just tow the rest to shore?"

"Yeah," I yelled back as if he was 50 feet away, not three. "Good idea, Ron. Good idea."

I turned the bow and began paddling through the foul flotsam surrounding us. There was a good 100 foot circle of smoking hide and mystery chunks and shocked fish.

I reached into the duffle bag and grabbed my rope, leaned forward, tapped Ron on the back and passed it to him slowly. One hand cupped behind his back, Ron took the line and I paddled him up to the smoking remains in silence.

Ron made a slip knot and attached it to the cow's remaining front leg. Then I turned the canoe around and tied the line to the gunwale. Ron picked up his paddle and we headed for shore.

But no matter how far we paddled from the explosion, we could not get away from the stink of rotting moose. I realized the explosion had driven the stench into our clothes and maybe even deep into our pores. I couldn't have smelled worse than if I had rolled in it.

Ron was paddling at a good clip from the bow position and I was working hard to keep up. Of course, every once in awhile we would have to steer around a chunk of moose in front of us or an old log that been dislodged from the pond bottom. Ron paused more than once to shake something pretty ugly off his paddle too. That slowed us down a bit. But we got to shore within a couple minutes.

We jumped up into the shallows and began brushing sticky little bits of moose from our hats, shirts and trousers. I wished I could just strip down and jump into the pond with a good bar of soap and a scrub brush.

But we still had the remnant cow carcass to handle. Ron and I dragged it onto shore and then towed it a good 40 feet back into the bushes. We decided to let the foxes, coyotes, crows and vultures enjoy the feast.

I wondered if they considered gunpowder a condiment.

We walked back to the canoe and splashed the

inside with clean pond water before our portage back. My duffle bag could wait for the garden hose at home.

Ron was unusually quiet. My ears were still ringing pretty bad. I suspected Ron's hearing was in a similar state. I chalked up his silence to us both being deaf, shell-shocked or both.

By the time we got back to the trucks and separated our gear, it was close to noon. I opened my truck door, saw my lunch bag and remembered I had packed two sandwiches, one for Ron and one for me.

"Hey Ron, you hungry? I packed a sandwich for you this morning." Ron looked briefly interested and started towards me and reached out his hand for the sandwich.

"It's moose," I said smiling as I held it out to him.

Ron looked like I had just insulted his mother.

He shook his head, turned away and walked briskly to his truck and jumped behind the wheel.

Gravel spit out from under the rear tires as he pulled onto the road.

I was still standing there holding the sandwich.

I saw Ron stick his arm out of the window and wave goodbye.

Anyway, I think it was a wave.

"A bison-sized creature in filthy long
johns flew out the window. His shoulder
slammed me in the face and pasted my
nose to my cheek as he sailed past.
I pulled my neck back into my collar like
a snapping turtle, but I was too late.
As a final insult, the suspect's toenails
clipped my chin."

GIMMEE THE GUN

"Lamoille 989."

Something about the crackle of my radio in the middle of the night that sends a Warden's pulse into overdrive—well, mine anyway.

I picked up the receiver and replied, "89 Lamoille."

"Shots fired over by Luke Hart's place," the Dispatcher said, and reading my mind, added, "The complainant didn't see anyone but figures someone is up to something."

Gotta love Vermont dispatchers. They tell it the way it is.

"10-4. I'm on my way."

I knew the guy. Luke was trouble. He was trouble for the police, trouble for us wardens

and trouble for his family. Luke was built
like a fire hydrant with a red face to match.
He was known for a bad attitude that got a lot
worse when he was drinking, and he drank a
lot. Even when he wasn't plastered, he used
his bulk and a permanent scowl to intimidate
people and get his way. When Luke walked
down the sidewalk in Hardwick, most people
quickly found a reason to cross the street.

He'd had many skirmishes with the law.

The deputy sheriffs and state police knew him
best as a source of domestic violence calls. A
family get together at Luke's just wasn't complete
until there were busted windows, broken
furniture, women screaming, kids crying and lots
of cruisers with blue lights shining in the yard.

Luke had spent a few nights in jail for drunken
driving, threatening people, and fencing stolen
goods. His wife and the mother to his half
dozen kids had left Luke years ago.

Luke's progeny were easy to spot around
town. They all had the same sandy colored
hair and freckles. Luke's boys had his square
head, broad shoulders and big chips on their
shoulders. Thumbs jammed into their jean
pockets, they didn't walk, they swaggered. His
girls were mostly quiet and shy with sad eyes.

Luke had inherited the place from his parents who had run a nice dairy farm until they passed away. But Luke had no interest in farming. He liked cars, fast ones. As soon as his parents were gone he sold all the cows, sold the milking equipment and started working on cars and trucks in the yard.

He was a self-trained auto mechanic, body paint and junk man who read survival magazines and went to Thunder Road every chance he got. His big dream was getting himself a car good enough to race himself.

Working out of his home—literally—there was no garage—his work hours were erratic, just like his life. Luke could be working hard on a vehicle or totally drunk at 2 pm or 2 am or any time in between.

Time didn't matter to him. This made Luke unpredictable and even more dangerous. Add guns to the mix and I could be driving right into trouble.

It was a half hour drive to the old farm. I had time to think about all this and more. But I also had to come up with a plan. I decided since there was shooting involved, I should play it cool. I needed to get close, then sit and listen out of sight but within earshot.

I didn't want to surprise Luke or whoever was doing the shooting and maybe become one of the targets.

I knew the hills surrounding Luke's home. I decided I would sit in my cruiser with the windows down and listen for a bit. If a shot was fired I'd be able to determine the approximate caliber. That and the direction someone was shooting and the frequency of the shots would all help build a case if there was one to be made.

As I turned down Luke's long private driveway, I turned off my headlights. About 800 feet from the house, at the top of a little rise, I rolled my window down and pulled off into the bushes, shut off the engine and just listened.

I waited a good twenty minutes and didn't hear a thing. I didn't see any lights shining either. It was 3 am. The woods were quiet except for an owl calling and a red fox trotting past my cruiser.

This impromptu stakeout appeared to be going nowhere. If Luke was poaching deer, maybe he was busy cutting it up. I slid out of my cruiser and took a little walk.

I wove my way through some trees until I could look down onto Luke's place with my binoculars. One light was burning inside the house—probably the kitchen. No noise was coming from the place. I stood silently and waited another half hour—listening for the sound of anyone moving around in the house or outbuildings. Nothing. If there had been gunshots, it was over.

Could be the caller was dead wrong about where the shots were coming from to begin with. Could be the caller had even mistaken firecrackers for what she heard for gunshots. Could be the call itself was a prank—a payback from one of the many folks who wanted to pay Luke back for something, or pay me back for that matter. I walked back to my cruiser.

I radioed Lamoille Dispatch and asked if there had been any more calls about shots fired since the original call nearly three hours earlier.

"Negative," the dispatcher said.

The sun would be coming up soon and it was time for me to move on before folks saw my cruiser on their commute to work. If I needed to conduct more stakeouts, I preferred to keep my surveillance patterns in the area to myself.

Three nights later, I got another complaint about "shots in the night time" in the same

general location. I headed back out to listen
and watch once again. It was closer to 1 am
this time. Maybe the earlier hour would help
me.

I parked the cruiser along the same old farm
trail, rolled down my window and listened.
Hearing nothing but the wind in the trees, I
grabbed my binoculars and with my pistol on
my hip headed up a ridge off to my left to get a
better look. The moon was waxing towards full
and there were just a few clouds in the sky. If
I was going to see movement outside the place,
this was the perfect night for it.

Hidden in an old sugarbush and courtesy of
the moonlight, I was able to look right down
on Luke's house, farm barn and outbuildings.
There were a dozen cars and trucks scattered in
Luke's yard. Some were parked with their grills
reaching for the sky like night feeding bass.
Luke had at least three of them up on blocks.
Others had their trunks popped open—handy
for tool storage while working under the hood
on the vehicle right behind it.

A newer Ford truck was sitting there with the
hood open as if Luke would be back any minute
now to finish the job. The moonlight bounced
off a silver box wrench lying right across the top
of the radiator.

There was knee high grass, parts of cars and garbage strewn about and the same single light on inside the house. I scanned my binoculars all across the yard and along the woods. There was no sign of movement.

I listened hard. Nothing.

I walked the hills surrounding the house. I spent a good two hours waiting for more shots to be fired anywhere in the area.

Nothing.

I sighed and walked back to the cruiser. I called into Dispatch and again reported no sign of any shooting or illegal activity and let her know I was headed home.

But on my drive home I decided maybe I was going about this wrong. Maybe I just needed to begin my surveillance earlier in the night.

I decided to call in my friend and fellow warden, John, for help. Together we could stake out Luke's place. If there really were shots being fired, it made sense to have two of us on the case anyway, I figured.

Forty-eight hours later, I had John riding shotgun in my cruiser. We were catching up on

pending cases when another call came over the
radio about shots being fired over near Luke's
place.

"Hey, our timing is right on," I grinned at John,
and pushed harder on the gas pedal.

"Guess you called this one right, Eric," John
agreed.

John is a rugged, reliable warden who used
more of a tough guy approach than I did. My
technique was more Jimmy Stewart while
John's was more John Wayne.

If Luke or someone else in the house was
poaching deer, he should have a freezer full by
now, I thought. But John and I both knew we
couldn't get a warrant to search the house on
suspicion alone. We needed evidence.

As we approached the crest of the hill above
Luke's place I slowed the cruiser and we rolled
down the windows. I looked at my watch. It
was a little after 11 pm, as we rolled on down to
my hidden parking spot.

We'd been parked barely five minutes,
formulating a plan to walk and scout the area
together, when we heard a shot. It appeared
to be a .30-.30. But had the shot come from

Luke's house or in the woods behind it?

Forget the stake out at the top of the hill. John and I knew we had to get as close to Luke's home as we could without being discovered. We needed to identify the shooter and his target.

We slid out of the cruiser and headed out down the drive towards the house in silence. The moon was waning and there were a lot of clouds. It's going to be tough to communicate if I lose sight of John, I was thinking to myself.

John and I scooted low alongside the battered trucks and cars in the yard, through belt high burdocks, milkweed and goldenrod. We would stop, wait and listen, then nod to each other and move off quietly again.

We were within 50 feet of the front door and about 10 feet apart when John stopped abruptly and looked over at me. He made a circling motion with one hand and looked away. I understood him to mean we should split off and meet out back. I nodded and peeled off in the opposite direction.

Luke's house was a big Federalist style home. It must have been quite a beauty in its day. But the last 50 years had not been kind. It was clear the house had been begging for a coat of paint for decades. The weathered clapboards were as curled and brittle as leaves in winter.

Just like the other nights, the one light was burning inside the house. I decided to head for it. Nice thing about this old house, it sported those huge six over six single pane original windows. Tough on the winter heating bill, but easy to see inside.

I ducked down and walked carefully over to the side of the house and got close to the room with the shining light. I poked my head up like a prairie dog and saw an old electric cooking stove and refrigerator. I'd been right about the location. It was Luke's kitchen. A single bulb hung from a bare socket connected to ancient knob and tube wiring.

Like a lot of old Vermonters, Luke probably just left the bulb burning all day and night in every season. It was a habit left over from the dairy farm, when milking started before dawn every morning and the evening milking finished in pitch black in January. Farm families learned it was just easier to let the bulb burn all day.

Looking a little closer at the room, I saw a big kitchen table covered in dirty dishes, stained coffee mugs and mounds of yellowing newspapers. There were a half dozen wooden kitchen chairs, none of which matched. They were tossed about the room just like the vehicles in the front yard—willy nilly. From the looks of the place, there wasn't a woman living there.

I saw a wall mounted phone and next to it, a fist sized hole and lathe and plaster chunks lying on the dirty linoleum below. Looked like someone had recently slammed a fist into the wall.

I leaned in closer to the glass and listened hard for any sound of people talking or footsteps or a radio or television chattering.

But all I heard was the sound of late summer crickets buzzing in the tall grass surrounding me.

I decided it was time to move on. The back corner of the house was less than 10 feet away. I had just begun to glide down when the shot went off.

BLAM!

What the ????

My heart jumped a good eight inches into my throat. I slammed my backside against the crumbling clapboards and dropped like a rock to the ground. I sat perched on my toes, drew my pistol and waited.

My ears were ringing. Where was John? Was he all right? I knew the sound of his revolver and it was not his gun that had fired.

I waited a few seconds, and then slunk further along the foundation.

I got to the corner, took a deep breath and peeked around the corner of the house with my revolver peeking too.

The clouds had lifted a little. I saw an open window just 10 feet away from me on the back of the house and a swaying rifle barrel sticking out of it—waving back and forth like an angry tiger's tail.

I peered hard into the darkness beyond the rifle barrel towards the weeds and tall grass looking for any sign of John. For once, it was a huge relief not to see him.

Whoever was waving that rifle barrel out the window apparently had no idea he had company coming. So far, so good.

I stayed crouched low at the corner of the house and waited for John to appear. I was some relieved when I spotted him. He was bent low at the opposite corner of the old house, hidden in the brush.

John was gesturing to me, like a catcher to a pitcher. He was making hand signals. Trouble was, I had no idea what John was trying to tell me.

The rifle barrel continued to sway up above and between us. I was concerned that if whoever was holding the weapon figured out we were here, we would be in real trouble.

I figured John would want us to back up and meet out front.

So, my jaw about hit the ground when I saw John begin to slowly duck walk in towards the open window. I looked harder and saw he still had his pistol in its holster.

My surprise turned to shock.

I had no idea what John's plan was, but I knew I needed to back him up. So, I dropped even lower and slid around the corner of the house, pointed my pistol at the window and crawled in closer to the shooter as well.

If the shooter heard us, lowered the muzzle and pulled the trigger, we wouldn't stand a chance.

We were about as close to sitting ducks as wardens could get.

I was praying that whoever was holding the rifle was hard of hearing.

It was a big house, but it didn't take but a half dozen stealthy steps for John and I to meet up beneath the open window. I crouched and waited. Goldenrod tickled my nose. John was maybe a yard from me.

I heard angry muttering up above. While I couldn't make out the words, it was a man's voice. The slurred speech made it clear whoever was holding the rifle had been holding a bottle or two earlier. This guy was plastered.

John looked at me and pointed his left index finger up into the air and nodded at me. All I could do was stare. I still had no idea what his game plan was.

"I'm ready," I was thinking.

But I wasn't.

Like a wide receiver leaping for the ball on a Hail Mary pass in the final seconds of the Super Bowl, John rocketed straight up and grabbed the rifle barrel in both hands. Then he twisted in the air and pulled forward hard, swinging the rifle over his head in a big wide arc, like he was splitting firewood.

I was so shocked, I jumped up.

Big mistake.

A bison-sized creature in filthy long johns flew out the window. His shoulder slammed me in the face and pasted my nose to my cheek as he sailed past. I pulled my neck back into my collar like a snapping turtle, but I was too late. As a final insult, the suspect's toenails clipped my chin.

I was rocked back on my heels and shaken up a bit.

Our gun wielding Tinkerbelle held on tight to the rifle a bit too long. He belly flopped into the pucker brush, his head went thump and he lay face down in a heap.

It took a second or two for my nose to settle back into the middle of my face and for my head to clear. I took a deep breath and looked over at John.

He had the rifle in his hands and was already busy emptying the chamber.

I holstered my pistol and grabbed my flashlight and turned it on. I said, "Freeze! Wardens!" I was trying hard to make myself useful.

But I quickly realized there was little chance this fellow would leap to his feet and pull a knife out of his skivvies. Our suspect was face down in the goldenrod and burdocks, not twitching so much as a finger. In fact, for a second I thought maybe we had scared him to death.

I looked over at John. He had ejected five rounds from the rifle's chamber and was sliding them into his pocket.

I looked back at the suspect. Was he breathing?

I heard a muffled, "Unh. What the ?" coming from the grass. I saw some burdock leaves begin to shake and knew our suspect was alive.

John laid the empty rifle up against the house a good distance away from where the fellow was flopped. Then we both went over to help him up.

The big lump of humanity struggled to roll over and look at us. There was a lot of spitting and sputtering and frog like leg movements. John and I looked at each other, nodded, then got him to his knees and finally to his feet. It was no easy task. The guy was 240 pounds or more and very inebriated.

"Luke?" I asked.

"Unh?" the figure answered.

I took that to be a yes.

"Game Wardens. We're here to talk to you about shooting at night."

"Uh," he said.

Once we had him on his feet, I cuffed his hands behind his back. His hands were huge, calloused and grimy. He reeked of sweat, gasoline, motor oil and booze.

"Anyone with you in the house tonight?" John asked him.

"Unh-unh," he said, shaking his head slowly side to side. John and I took him at his word but we knew to keep an eye out for signs to the contrary.

"You expecting anyone?" John added.

Luke's head was wobbly and he swayed like a willow tree. "Nah," he grunted.

John escorted Luke into the house while I took my flashlight and walked off into the overgrown meadow and along the woods to scout for dead or wounded deer.

I couldn't find any evidence of deer having been shot. I walked back to the house and into the kitchen where John was standing. Luke was seated at the table, swaying, with his head bent low, his eyes mostly shut.

I asked Luke what he was shooting at night.

Luke's head bobbled a bit on his shoulders. He looked up at me as if I was an idiot and said, "Leaves."

Well, there wasn't a closed season on leaves. And what he didn't hit with lead, Mother Nature would knock to the ground in another month or so with a killing frost.

"Mind if we look in your freezer and take a look around the house?" I asked.

Luke grunted his approval. His head fell back to his chest, his eyelids struggled to stay open.

John stayed with Luke while I took a quick look inside. There was no evidence of deer having been recently taken and cut up.

I walked back into the kitchen and gave John my report.

Luke was falling asleep in the chair and in danger of tumbling over. I noticed he had an egg growing on his forehead from where he had hit the ground too.

"Anyone living here with you?" John asked him.

"Nah. Kids gawn," he said. Then in a voice as soft as a 16 year-old boy who had his heart broken for the first time, he said, "She lev me too." His shoulders began to shake and tears began rolling down his cheeks. He launched into a lament about a woman.

John and I looked at one another. It appeared this terror of the Northeast Kingdom was heart broken.

This was turning into a social work call. It was clear to us the best thing for Luke was sleep.

Unable to find any evidence of poaching, I hid the emptied rifle in a corner of a distant room behind some curtains where it would be days, maybe months before Luke would find it.

John went and got the remaining box of ammo from the bathroom where Luke had been firing into the backyard and pocketed all the shells.

We didn't want Luke having a rifle or any guns about when he was so inebriated and worse, depressed about some woman. Right now his alleged target was leaves, but that might change if he didn't get out of this funk.

John and I lectured Luke briefly. I told him he couldn't continue shooting at night. He was disturbing the peace, a crime. If we had to come back, we would take his rifle, give him a citation and he would end up in court.

He asked who we were. He muttered something about angles, which made no sense to me. We told him we were wardens, but it didn't appear to stick. He said, "I'm sorry. I didn't mean it. I didn't mean it," a few times. Then I saw tears streaming down his cheeks.

He was off in a big boozy world of hurt. We were done.

John and I helped Luke to bed. The springs groaned as he fell onto the covers. He asked one last time, "Who are you guys? Are you angles?"

I finally got it. Luke was trying to say "angels" but he was so drunk his tongue tripped on the "g."

Luke closed his eyes and passed out.

I looked at John and asked, "You figure we've done about all we can do here tonight?"

"Guess so," John agreed.

We left the house as we found it, with the kitchen light on and the bathroom window open. Back at the cruiser, I asked John, "You think Luke will remember any of this tomorrow?"

"I doubt it," John said, paused and chuckled. "If we had cited him, he never would have found it in that pile on his kitchen table anyway. Let's just hope we don't have to come back. I'm not sure I could jump like that again."

Days passed and then weeks went by with no more complaints about Luke. I kind of forgot about him.

But as ever, I kept my ear to the ground and in among the stories I was hearing, were a few good ones about Luke.

Folks told me the rusted cars and trucks scattered across Luke's front lawn had been hauled away to a crusher. His front and back lawn had been mowed—well, brush hogged anyway. And the biggest change of all was that Luke was said to be on the wagon. This news was widely cheered by law enforcement in the greater Hardwick area.

The following June, I saw Luke in a clean shirt and trousers attending the high school graduation of one his kids. There was a woman about his age sitting beside him. I was not in uniform and it was clear he didn't recognize me.

Later that same summer I spotted Luke at a creemee stand buying a couple freckle-faced kids ice cream cones. His scowl was gone and the kids looked happy to be with him.

Over the next couple of years, life only got better for Luke. He got a steady job in town as a mechanic fixing exhausts and replacing brakes. He was seen cheering at his kids' baseball games and in the audience applauding them when they appeared in school plays and choirs.

Luke had become respectable.

The timing of Luke's transformation was pretty remarkable and I've always wondered about it. Did John and I play a part in Luke rejoining society?

Did Luke really believe John and I were "angles"

as he said that night? Angels who had lifted him up and thrown him down—smote him as it were—and scared him into changing his ways?

Or maybe you could rationalize it another way—go purely with science. Maybe Luke's midnight flight into the pucker brush rattled his brain just enough to promote positive changes in his behavior. They say that can happen too.

Or was it all just pure coincidence?

I know game wardens aren't social workers and I can't prove John's gutsy gun barrel grab was the impetus for one notorious Northeast Kingdom outlaw to sober up and rejoin society.

But stranger things have happened up here.

**"So I turned my head to the left a bit
and yelled, 'John, you cover me,'
as if I had a partner up in the
darkness backing me up."**

Cover Me

Maybe taking fish or game out of season becomes an adrenalin rush for some folks. I don't know.

I do know that poachers are tough to catch and it can take many sleepless, cold nights sitting still in the woods to gather evidence, and if you are lucky, to catch 'em red handed.

Most of the time it is a phone call that sets a warden to watching a particular meadow or clearing deep in the woods off an old logging trail.

Ironically, my best tipsters were often retired poachers. Too arthritic or tired to get back into the woods and poach themselves, they still had friends or sons and grandsons of these old friends who had a taste for venison in any season and no respect for the law.

So, it was that I got a call from Joe—a local in

his late 70's who had been cited more than once for hunting game out of season. For whatever reason, Joe was on the straight and narrow now and like a reformed smoker, he couldn't stand tobacco use—or in this case, poaching. He was one of my best informants.

"You might want to keep an eye on the big meadow off Codding Hollow Road in Waterville," Joe said. "Some guys are bragging they have already taken two deer off that piece this summer. Huntin' it late at night."

I didn't ask for details. It is against the code to ask for specifics. Joe probably knew exactly who these fellows were. Heck, they might even be relatives of his. It was not uncommon for a poacher to turn in his own relatives if there was a family feud going on. Up here a lot of the folks are related. And like the saying goes, familiarity can breed contempt.

One of these fellows must have really upset Joe.

I knew Joe well enough to believe him. He had given me solid leads before. So here I was stashing my truck off behind some pines maybe 15 feet alongside a nice big meadow. It should have a lot of deer feeding here come the middle of the night. I was waiting—just as I had the five nights before this one, when I first got Joe's call.

I parked my truck just far enough into the woods where I could look the meadow.

I draped a camo cover over the truck to hide my presence.

I ran my conversation with Joe over in my head again. I was beginning to wonder if Joe had lied to me. But I told myself a few more sleepless nights wouldn't hurt. I could play the radio low and listen to ballgames while keeping watch.

Trouble was, the Red Sox game on WDEV had been over for about four hours and the warden radio had been silent for an hour or more too. Most of Vermont's residents were home in a nice warm bed. I had made about as many "Honey do" lists in my head as I could. I was about out of deep thoughts and had run out of shallow ones a long time ago. It was pitch dark and I could see my breath. The coffee in my thermos was as cold as iced tea.

Well, at least the mosquitoes weren't biting.

It was then I saw a beam of light shining in the meadow directly below and in front of me maybe

200 yards away. I watched carefully as the light traveled the entire length of the meadow and the beam swung back and forth around deer head height. It was headed right for me.

No one could walk or run that fast and swing the beam in a nice smooth arc. So that meant at least two guys headed towards me, shining their light on the same side of the road as me.

I hoped I'd done a good job with the camo.

Most deer jackers use spotlights or their car headlights to light up the field and then shoot at the reflecting eyes of the deer. Deer are mesmerized by the lights and generally don't spook. Once shot, it is a matter of running, most often with a buddy or two, getting the deer into your vehicle as fast as you can and driving off before someone reports you.

I rolled my window down to listen. I waited and watched and held my breath. I did not want to chance getting out in case the door hinges squeaked or they heard the door latch pop. I heard the sound of tires on gravel traveling at a crawl towards me. I saw the light swing wide along the meadow getting closer and closer to the tree line and me.

I waited to see if that swinging beam would lock

on my truck. If it did, if they spotted me and took off, I needed to be ready for a chase.

Just ten yards from my truck the spotlight went dark.

I held my breath for a second as their truck rolled slowly by me. Only the parking lights were shining. I guessed these fellows must not have seen any deer in the meadow, so they were off to find another that might give them a chance to blind a deer and shoot it.

I couldn't see much, but the vehicle appeared to be a dark colored pickup with a cap. Driving with his headlights off was more evidence that whoever was in that truck was up to no good.

As soon as they went by me, I popped my truck door, jumped out of the cab and scooted to the road to try and get their license plate number. No luck. It was bent and torn and covered with mud. I could see it was a faded Vermont plate, that was about all.

I decided to try and follow them in my truck while keeping my distance. I ran back to my truck, yanked the camo cover off, stuffed it in the truck bed and jumped back in the cab. I quietly shut the truck door, turned on the engine and rolled out of my hiding place nice and slow. I couldn't see their truck, but figured it was ahead. I kept my driver's window down and leaned my head out, listening as best I could for the sounds of gunshots up ahead.

The problem was I knew there were no more meadows up ahead. It was all woods on both sides of this typical Vermont hill and dale curved dirt road. Worse, it ended at a crossroad about a quarter mile ahead. If these fellows were intent on shining and shooting into old pastures and meadows, I had no idea where they were going. The best deer meadows were behind us.

Once they got to the end of the road, they would have to turn right or left. Would I be able to see their tracks?

I was also more than a little concerned the crew in that truck might be looking for a place to turn around. If that were the case, I'd meet them coming back at me—both of us crawling along with our lights off on this narrow dirt road around 3 am.

There was nowhere for me to hide if that happened. They would be spooked and all my sleepless nights would be for nothing. Still, I had to take a chance and keep following.

At the T, I jumped out of my truck to look at the tire tracks on the dirt road.

I saw that some vehicles had recently turned down the hill toward the main road. But I figured no way this crew was going to drive down a paved road with their headlights off, where they might run into a state trooper asking questions or nosey neighbors who might call the police and report them.

I looked both ways and could not see any tail lights shining ahead of me. The clock was ticking. I knew if I went one way it would be the wrong way and if I went the other, I might actually catch up to them and blow the whole investigation when they spotted me. I stepped farther away from the truck and listened hard.

If I could just witness these fellows shining their light on another field or two, even if they didn't take a deer, I would have a good case under Vermont law. But all I had now, after five nights of sitting and waiting, was suspicious behavior.

Time to give up and go home.

I circled slowly around and aimed my grill back up the road where I had lost their license plate lights. I turned my headlights on, figuring I was

done for the night and my suspects were long
gone.

I hadn't driven more than 100 yards up the
road when I saw it—fresh vehicle tracks leading
into a little used dirt trail on my right. The tall
grass was still bent down. I knew from my years
patrolling the area that this private road led to
an abandoned farmhouse surrounded by acres
of overgrown hay fields and cow pasture just a
few hundred feet away. The trees were growing
in thick, but it was still passable to someone
who had a good four wheel drive truck and
didn't care if their paint got scratched up a bit.

I'd been so intent on trying to figure out which
way the truck would turn at the end of the road
that I forgot about this driveway. Now that I had
my headlights on, I could see it.

Had someone been visiting the place earlier
in the day or did those tracks belong to my
suspects? Maybe I hadn't missed them at the
end of the road after all. Maybe they'd turned
in here before they ever got to the T. These guys
might be shining a light and aiming at a deer
right now.

With my left hand, I killed all my truck lights
and with my right hand I spun the steering

wheel like a ship's wheel and rolled over the fresh tracks and into the brush.

I didn't go but a few feet before I turned off the engine. I didn't know how far up the drive they were—if they were there—and I didn't want to surprise anyone carrying guns. As quietly as I could, I opened my door and stepped out. My pistol was on my hip. I leaned over and grabbed my flashlight, then I started walking slow up the rutted drive.

I walked maybe 50 feet through a canopy of saplings before I saw it—the same dark colored pickup truck parked in the dooryard of an abandoned farmhouse.

What were they up to?

The glass was mostly shot out of the old house and the porch roof had fallen in making it about impossible to get to the front door. The house had been empty for at least a decade. So these fellows sure weren't calling on anyone at this hour. And if they were real estate agents, it was a little early in the day for a showing.

There was no sound coming from the truck. I wondered if they had heard me driving by in the dark? Were they on to me? Is that why they pulled in here? Or did they just pull off to have a smoke and a beer and to plan their next move? Or maybe they were off out back shining a light and I couldn't see them? A lot of possibilities ran through my head.

Just then I saw two guys walk around the front of the truck. One opened the passenger door and pulled out two rifles, handing one to the other fellow. Then they shut the door, turned and headed away from me again.

I crouched down in the tall grass and burdocks, less than 100 feet away from the truck. I counted a slow minute after they headed out. Then I stood up, listened hard and began following them. I wanted to see what had their interest at 4 am.

On the backside of the old farmhouse was a large field. One of the men was sweeping a strong white light slowly across it. He would shine the light for maybe 15 seconds and then shut it off. The next time the light came on, he would have moved 50 feet or more. He seemed to have broken the field up into a pie shape. I figured he thought he would be less likely to spook grazing deer this way. I could see whatever he was up to, he would be at it awhile.

I decided I had time to scoot back to their truck and check it out.

I wanted to know what these fellows had in there for a potential arsenal if I decided to introduce myself.

I peeked inside while shining my light and saw a typical woodchuck decorated interior. There were lots of empty beer bottles and cans on the floor along with candy wrappers, fast food boxes and other stuff scattered about. The cab smelled like stale beer. Of most interest to me was a half filled box of some pretty heavy duty ammo boasting hollow points. These boys had the tools to do some real damage if they didn't like it when I introduced myself.

They were pretty well armed and had probably been drinking too. A bad combination. I looked at the ignition and sure enough, they had left the keys hanging there. I leaned in the open driver's window, pulled the keys out and dropped them into my breast pocket.

We were going to have a little talk when they got back if we didn't run into each other sooner. I didn't want my truck grill smashed by them throwing their rig in reverse and slamming into it. Worse, if they got past my vehicle somehow,

I could have a chase on my hands. Pocketing their keys meant the only race we might have would be on foot. And if that happened, my money would be on me.

I walked back to the meadow, sticking to the tall grass and winding my way through the saplings and into the tree line slightly above and behind the pair. They were still busy doing that same light shining pattern. The one fellow with the light had his rifle on a sling over his shoulder. The other fellow was off to the side a good 25 feet, rifle in his arms ready to raise and fire. I stood watching the pair maybe 20 minutes when the light went off for good and I saw them walk up to each other and have a brief discussion. I couldn't hear a word. Then I saw them turn and start walking back towards the old farmhouse, on their way to their truck and past me.

Just then it hit me that I had two well armed, disappointed, possibly pretty beered up poachers coming my way who were going to be even less happy when they couldn't find their truck keys.

I had to think fast. I didn't want to have a shoot out but I wasn't about to let them get away without a little chat either. While they were crossing the field about 300 feet below me, I trotted ahead through the trees as quietly as I could to beat them back to their truck. If they heard me and that fellow with the spotlight got me locked in his beam, I would be in real trouble.

I made it back to their truck and crouched behind the driver's side door. I unholstered my pistol. When I heard their boots scuffing through the tall grass, I stood up and leaned over the hood of their truck. I leveled my .357 Smith & Wesson at them and turned my flashlight on. I shouted out, "Game Warden, don't move!"

You'd have thought Bigfoot had just risen up.

Their eyes and mouths fell wide open. One of them yelped like a puppy and stopped so short he stumbled and fell to his knees.

"Put your guns on the ground—now!" I said with authority.

They laid their rifles down. "All right, now put your hands behind your heads and walk on in here nice and slow."

As they began to walk towards me it struck me that if they knew I was alone, they might just figure one or both of them could make a run for it and get away.

So I turned my head to the left a bit and yelled, "John, you cover me," as if I had a partner up in the darkness backing me up.

So far so good. They were doing what I told them to do. Now for the tricky part, when they figured out that John didn't exist.

I kept the light trained on the pair, quietly holstered my pistol and reached for the handcuffs. Darn. I'd only brought one set of cuffs. The spare was hanging back in my truck.

Still standing behind my light, I stepped a few feet behind and to the left of the hood and said, "Step up here slowly and put your wallets on the hood of the truck and empty your pockets." If they decided to run for it, I'd have their ID and their truck.

I was trying to move things along quickly before they realized I was alone talking to them. So far they had not said a word or asked about John.

I wished a fox or some animal would run behind me in the woods so they might think the noise was coming from my imaginary partner.

The pair of them was standing there in front of me. The only thing between us was their truck. I made certain to be out of reach if they decided to lunge for me.

"Now put your hands palm down on the truck hood, spread wide and stay put. You're both under arrest."

Neither one of these guys said a word. Maybe the beer and the late hour were having an effect. Maybe they thought I was Bigfoot. I moved behind the biggest guy, and told him to put his hands behind his back slowly, one by one, and cuffed him. I told the other fellow to keep his hands on the hood.

Then I came around in front of the pair, off to the side and gathered up their wallets, some shells, loose change, a pocket knife and other junk they had spread on the truck hood and put it all in an evidence bag. They still weren't talking.

Well, that's just as well, I thought. It was my turn after five nights of sitting alone in my truck.

I told them they were being cited into court for attempting to spot and locate deer at night. This woke them up.

Both of them started protesting and making up stories about why there were out there shining a light. Problem was their stories didn't match and they were contradicting each other right there in front of me and starting to argue.

I began to write each of them up. When they realized they were not going to leave without citations, the shorter fellow said, "This just ain't right. I want to talk to that other warden. John is it? Hey, John!" he shouted up into the dark.

Well that kind of put me in a bad spot. I sure wished I had watched those old Charlie McCarthy shows a bit closer. I might be able to throw my voice behind me somehow like a ventriloquist. But I don't think even the best Vegas act could have thrown their voice 40 plus feet back into the trees.

I had to act fast to diffuse this guy.

"Hey! You can tell it to the judge. Just be quiet and you will be on your way home soon. If you two want to keep talking, I will take you both in."

It worked. They shut up. I wrote each of them up and then walked around to the back of the big guy and unlocked his cuffs. I stepped back behind the hood and handed them their citations. I tucked their licenses in my jacket. Then I picked up their rifles, the spotting light and ammo.

I turned and shouted over my shoulder, "John, I'm good. You can head on back to the truck. I'll meet you there."

I wished I had a bear up there to grunt, a buck to snort or some sort of animal to go busting back through the trees or make some noise behind me. But again, I decided to just keep forging ahead and not give these fellows time to think about my silent partner.

"All right, Gentlemen. Your rifles, light and licenses are coming with me. John and I are parked behind your truck. You just wait here five minutes for us to back our truck out of this lane and then you head on home. I will be in touch." I laid their truck keys on the hood.

Maybe they were tired. Maybe they figured John was a native tracker or so omnipotent he could not be seen or heard. For whatever reason they were compliant. I got out of there that night safe and sound.

Most folks plead no contest. So these guys surprised me when they hired an attorney and insisted on a trial by jury.

It is tough getting any Vermont jury to convict on fish and game violations unless the evidence of wrongdoing is compelling and rock solid. In this case, I didn't have a dead deer or so much as a fresh hide or blood evidence and deer hair in the back of the truck. I couldn't even say I had seen them shining a light on a deer, let alone that I had witnessed either man take a shot.

Add to this, the fact the rural Vermont is still a place where most everyone knows everyone else or worse, is related by blood or marriage.

So, while I knew what those good old boys were up to that night, I wasn't at all certain a jury would agree with me.

I prepared for a tough case. The defendants' attorney argued that his clients were out coon hunting that night and had lost their dogs. They were driving the back roads with the lights off and stopping at open areas to shine the light hoping to find their lost dogs, he said.

This was indeed a good story. The only problem was neither of them had been sharp enough to think of this story when I nabbed them about six months earlier.

With the help of the prosecutor I told the jury

just that. I also pointed out they didn't have any hunting dog gear in their truck. There wasn't a leash or a collar in the truck nor did a leash or collar land on the hood of the truck when they emptied their pockets in front of me.

They were also carrying high powered rifles used in deer hunting, not lighter caliber guns used for raccoon hunting. Nor did they ever call or whistle for their dogs any of the time they were scouting either field or driving the roads—as I would have heard them. Also, hounds make a racket. I would have heard the dogs running and barking in the woods, if they had been within a mile or two. Tough to miss a couple howling coon dogs. The jury laughed with me on this one. I thought I was making progress.

The State's Attorney brought all of this out in my testimony as he made his case against these two defendants. When we had heard what the defense was going to be, I had worked with the prosecutor preparing a list of questions for him to ask me.

Finally, it was time for the Defense Attorney to try and poke holes in my testimony. He went through a long review of my expertise and background and character. You could see him winding up like a pitcher in the final game of the World Series with the bases loaded and the home team down by one. Everyone was leaning in to see what he was about to pitch—the jury, the judge, the defense attorney, his clients and me. Here was his release:

"Warden Nuse, isn't it true that everything you saw the defendants doing in the field during the night in question was consistent with them looking for something?"

"Yes, Sir," I nodded. Then I looked directly at the jury and said, "DEER. That's why I cited them."

The jury sat back and roared. The judge bowed his head to stifle a chuckle. The defendants' shoulders sagged and their chins about hit the perfectly polished table.

I felt like I was in a boxing ring and I just landed a good one.

The Defense Attorney scowled and walked over to confer with his clients. He rifled through a few papers to buy some time. I noticed the pair were not looking as cocky as they had when the trial started.

After a minute or so, the attorney turned back towards me, cleared his throat, threw back his shoulders and fired another couple of questions at me. They didn't amount to much.

I glanced over at the jury. I had a sense they were with me on this one.

A few minutes later, the Defense rested and the jurors went off to deliberate. In less than an hour they were back with their verdict: guilty.

I'd put a lot of time into the case and was happy to win it.

I was even happier the Defense never called on John to testify about what he saw that night.

ACKNOWLEDGEMENT

*This book could not have been completed
without the encouragement and skill
of the following individuals:*

*Jean Pamela Poland, Dorrice Hammer,
Beth O'Keefe, Ingrid Nuse,
Carrie Cook and O.C.*

Thank you one and all.

Eric Nuse, our story teller, circa 1988.

Who We Are

Megan Price is a former award-winning journalist and Vermont legislator who knows a good story when she hears one.

Eric Nuse worked 32 years as a game warden in Vermont and never lost his sense of humor.

Bob Lutz worked 23 years as a warden in Vermont. He was last seen sewing fishing nets in Fiji.

Carrie Cook is an exceptional graphic designer and musician who lives in Cambridge, Vermont.

Want *MORE great stories?*
*Read **Volume Two** yet?*
Here's what you're missing:

4WD

STOWE TURKEY

TICK TRAIL

SATAN SERIES:

BLAME THE NAME?
THAT'LL TEACH HIM
DOG FISH
STAY
WRONG IS RIGHT

FLY TRAP

TRACK STAR

HARD TIMES

SEARCH WARRANT

HAVIN' HER SAY

SKINNY GOOSE

Volume Three coming soon...

Visit us at www.VermontWild.com